Airbags

and

Starting Over

A Personal Journey

Karen Pivott

https://www.amazon.com/author/karenpivott

BY THE SAME AUTHOR

BOOKS ON KINDLE

NON FICTION

Airbags and Starting Over

Back On the Road Again

Always Travel With Your Basket

CHILDRENS FICTION

Birthdays at the Bay

Royce and Billy

FICTION

By Any Other Circumstances

Create Space Publishing

4900 LaCross Road
North Charleston, SC 29406
USA

First Printing, Create Space 2016

ISBN-9780473273033

Published in New Zealand

FOREWORD

I hope this book will help you to see that an ordinary person has managed significant change to improve her own life and share how that in turn has improved the lives of others.

I have overcome a negative pattern of thinking and action and I believe we are never too old to know and experience success.

Change is not something to be feared, it can be good and used for good for yourself and others.

If you want to experience some tangible change in your life read on ......

Contents

ACKNOWLEDGMENTS

I acknowledge here that my journey has not been endured alone. Without my husband Alan and his ongoing support my books would not be possible. He has encouraged me and loved me throughout all the change, expected and unexpected.

I also would like to acknowledge my proof reader and friend Angela Rusk who pushed me onward and upward until I had completed my goal, along with my other supporters. Thank you all.

Chapter 1. The accident

It had been a full and productive day at work. A paperwork day. One of those days when you decide yes I have to do something about this mess on my desk and get the filing sorted before the end of year reporting next month.

November 18th 2010 which was also our wedding anniversary. Thirty two years of marriage and we had decided because it fell on a week day that we would celebrate our anniversary on the Saturday by having dinner at our favourite restaurant just out of town near the beach at "The Cabbage Tree". I had made the reservation weeks earlier.

So after a productive day and it being our regular fortnightly shopping day we set off leaving home at around 5.00 pm and making our way in the general direction of the supermarket when our trip was unceremoniously interrupted by a vehicle failing to give way at the give way sign and us driving straight into the side of him. In other words we 'T Boned' him. After unclipping my seat belt, I was aided from the vehicle by my husband Alan and the driver of the other vehicle, who pried my passenger door open. Upon alighting I noticed the airbags had deployed I had no memory of that happening at the time of impact. My fingers were swelling and my hands were tingling. I removed my rings and kept saying "I'm okay but what's wrong with my hands?"

The police were called and attended. They took statements and drove us home.

In the early hours of the morning I was woken by breathing difficulties and tremendous pain in both my hands and fingers. I got up gingerly and went into our lounge. I sat in my lazy boy with a pillow behind my head and a blanket over me. My feet were up and I sat dozing on and off until my husband got up.

I asked him to take me to the hospital.

We went to the local hospital in Invercargill and I was seen by a doctor there who said, "Thank the Lord you were wearing your seat belt." Upon examination multiple contusions was written on the Accident Compensation Form. I was given Ibuprofen and sent home on a five day medical certificate. When I asked about my hands I was told that was due to the Airbag deploying as was my breathing difficulty." You shouldn't breathe in when they go off." I was told by the doctor which given I have no memory of them deploying did not seem relevant advice to me, but now you the reader know, that if you are in an accident and the airbag deploys don't breathe. The reality is of course you are in an accident. You have just been hit by or hit a vehicle and the first thing you do is take a deep breath it is a natural response. It is automatic. Reactionary. You don't think about it. It is involuntary.

This accident changed my perception of life and my role in it. It was as if scales literally had fallen from my eyes and a barrier had fallen away, leaving only a protective cushion of learned life skills. Love and faith were really all that remained.

Facing loss

I went back to work. I got the bus one way with Alan picking me up at the end of my working day. I did not go back to full days which was a great help.

I lost my mother less than a month later to cancer. I had a replacement vehicle two days before her death enabling my husband and I to drive up to Auckland for her funeral some 1800 kilometers away. Flights in the month of December were cost prohibitive, and the reality for me was that I would need to have some of Mum's possessions to be sent down or picked up at a later stage. It was prudent to book the ferry and drive up which we did.

My boss Isabel with her number two Janice paid a surprise visit and brought a lovely toiletries gift for me which was extremely thoughtful.

Alan booked the ferry, we packed and left.

Did I cry all the way up? No. Mum had lived and left us the way she wanted. I spoke to her everyday on the phone even when her speech was strained I knew she knew what I was saying and she communicated well saying what she needed to, to me.

She told me "Be careful when you come up look where I am," in her slurred slow speech now very much becoming her normal speech, and as a dutiful daughter I assured her I would.

Our Christmas went from a pre-planned surprise for both our mother's to a non-event

4

in the celebratory sense.

We had a safe trip to Auckland. We had as my sister called it "a successful event on the day" and there were so many people there.

When my boss Isabel and her number two Janice arrived at our home prior to us leaving I received a phone call from my sister asking about numbers for catering purposes at the funeral. We had a rather stilted conversation about this I mean between us over the last fifteen years we had taken mum to many funerals of friends, acquaintances, neighbours, committee members, church members. Mum had led a full life and been a very social person so based on the funerals we had attended we estimated about eighty people and this was on the rather generous side. We decided to cater for one hundred so we could take leftovers home for the family who would stay into the evening.

The funeral home chapel was very full and just over one hundred people turned up. People that we knew from many years before, but didn't factor into our equation at all.

If there is one thing we have learned from this always expect the unexpected when involved with planning a funeral.

First Christmas

We spent Christmas Day with Alan's mum and Aunt and had a very good and relaxing day. We were quite tired so that was just what the doctor ordered.

We spent Boxing Day with my sister and her partner, my aunt and uncle and one of our nephews. We had a great day, lots of laughs, lots of good memories recalled and some tears.

Tears are something which rained down the mobile phone to my landline from Australia where my primary school friend Vanessa now living in England was on holiday, with the third member of our group Theresa (Tess) who now resides in New South Wales. I had told them both by email that mum had had a stroke and things were not looking good. Mobile numbers were exchanged. The days limped along and then a major set-back for mum which ultimately resulted in her death and my phone call to the 'girls'.

No matter how close you are to people emotionally I can tell you the geographical distance creates a space which may as well be one of infinity. No amount of consoling words, or tears can replace a hug, and when I phoned them I just wanted to be able to put my arms around them. We had spent so many hours together with Mum the three of us. Peeling peaches, then apples at preserving time. Cutting up vegetables for large pots of vegetable soup in the winter. Going on holidays together and long drives to the beach on weekends.

Vanessa who was coming to New Zealand after leaving Australia her partner Mike, myself and Alan met at the Southern Motorway for a coffee. I can tell you it was the longest coffee I have ever had and our two men were great about it. It had been thirty four years since we had been in the same room, but it was as yesterday. Vanessa and Theresa gave me some money to buy a plant for mum and I decided there and then that I would add some money to that amount and have a potted memorial garden for mum in our backyard.

When we parted Alan and I went to the Waikato to spend time with each of our children and their respective children our grandchildren.

All the adults were flat. It is fair to say that Christmas 2010 wasn't one of our most joyous, however through this period we felt, exchanged and shared in lots of love.

We saw 2011 in while we were in the Waikato and began to make our way home to Invercargill in early January. Alan had to go back to work and on our return home there was more news the farm where Alan worked was on the market and subsequently Alan was to be made redundant.

I returned to work and in March we flew up North to see our eldest son married. This was a joyous event and we all let our hair down and made the most of it. There were lots of laughs, lots of cooperation prior to the actual wedding day, lots of dancing and tears of a different kind.

On returning home Alan's redundancy became a reality and we prepared for another adjustment and that's when it happened.

I literally stopped one day and looked around me, at my surroundings, at where I was in life and decided I wanted more, I deserved more and I was going to have more.

That decided there was only one small glitch, I had absolutely no idea how I was to achieve all those things and right at that moment I didn't care. I just knew with certainty that somehow I would and so my journey began.........

I began by looking for all the good things that happened in a day. The smiles on people's faces, the flowers in gardens that should have finished a month before, the green lushness of the grass that was being mowed fortnightly a feat quite unusual for Invercargill at that time of the year.

Change and my world view

I started going to our local church and Alan began coming along as well. It had been years since we had gone to church and although the services weren't quite what we were used to the sermons were good and the people friendly. As we went more often I realised I actually knew a few of the Parishioners through my work.

I was becoming more aware than usual of things people were saying and I would act on things more readily. An example of this was when one of my work colleagues told me she had been to a Psychic in town after some thought I made an appointment and paid her a visit.

I was thinking along particular lines when I went there, and there were a few questions I had answered, but the amazing thing was that she addressed areas in my life that I wasn't consciously thinking of. Through her I learned about the book "The Secret" by Rhonda Byrne and I ordered a copy through the library. I had heard of this book before but never done anything about it.

9

When the book arrived I began reading it and realised that what I had started doing myself was not only endorsed by the book but encouraged.

I have since bought this book, and its sequel "The Power". Through these books I learned to want without guilt and raise my expectations of what is possible.

This is an irony in life for me. My vocation is as a Workplace Tutor my disciplines are Literacy and Numeracy with some computer skills thrown into the mix. I am always encouraging my learners to expect more and rise to the challenge. I will say here that this has never been a mantra. I truly believe that one of the big issues for people with literacy difficulties is their belief that they are either dumb and won't be any better, or that even when their literacy improves they are stuck where they are.

In my personal life I hadn't realised that I too was settling for what I had and ignoring what I wanted.

Engaging people, earning their trust and respect and helping them to achieve their goals, and empowering them are realities of the job I do. I am proud of that. It is achieved after many hours of work for both myself and the learner.

What I realised though is that I myself didn't have anyone to engage, encourage or empower me I was all there was and my expectations were lacking.

I decided to change this. I raised my expectations for myself and things in my world slowly began to change.

I expected positive people to come into my life, and they started arriving. I expected positive conversations with our children and they too began to happen. I expected more money to come in and less money to go out. I focused on more money coming in and I found that by focusing on what was coming in, the bills began to reduce. The phone bill was less, the power bill increase wasn't as large as we had been led to believe it would be. The grocery bill was under budget every shop, sometimes by a few dollars and sometimes by tens of dollars.

I was able to donate to one of my nominated charities and felt a great sense of joy as I posted this off. Was it hundreds? Thousands? No but it was something and I knew that something would be put to good use. Someone would benefit greatly from a little something extra and I was pleased to be able to give it.

There really is something rewarding about giving. I give in my job to others every day and what I have learned is that the more I give the more I receive. I teach my learners and I often get taught things by my learners.

I am open to good things. I am grateful for things. I take nothing for granted and I look for the good in people, situations, and places.

I don't just feel blessed each day. I know and believe I am blessed each and every day.

One of my active realisations is "Accept what you can't change". I don't get negative or frustrated I just accept without judging and remind myself of all the good things in my life.

I am pleased to say the list is getting longer and longer every day.

Now you may ask what has that to do with airbags.

Well airbags impact so quickly you are unaware they have struck you. Judging people can be like that. Before you know it you are in a conversation and your take on that person is over riding the facts, and you are quite often getting swept along with the conversation and not thinking too much about what you are saying.

Short everyday phrases can set the tone for negative conversation which can and often leads into a spiral of discussion which can make you feel better for a short period of time, but unfortunately at the expense of others.

Here is an example "Hi Jason."

"Pam. Isn't the weather awful?"

"Mr. Jenkins said the same thing to me yesterday."

"Mr. Jenkins. It wouldn't make any difference to him would it? He stays home playing with his models all day. He never thinks to go out for his wife, poor woman got absolutely drenched yesterday."

So let's have a look at what has occurred here.

"Hi Jason." A good greeting nothing wrong with this is there?

"Pam. Isn't the weather awful?" On the surface this seems a harmless response but let's look at this objectively. What is actually happening? The weather is being criticised. Criticism is a negative act.

"Mr. Jenkins said the same thing to me yesterday." A polite exchange has now begun.

Pam is now buying into the conversation.

"Mr. Jenkins. It wouldn't make any difference to him would it? He stays home playing with his models all day. He never thinks to go out for his wife, poor woman got absolutely drenched yesterday."

The conversation has now taken a dramatic turn for the worse. It has gone from criticising the weather to criticising and putting down Mr. Jenkins as well as judging him ' He never thinks to go out for his wife'.

My point here is to illustrate how easily we can get caught up in responding in an inappropriate way by that I mean we haven't thought about what has been said we are reactive, responsive not thinking about what we are saying.

This happens across families, in workplaces, across communities the world over and no good actually comes from it.

Let's look at the conversation again:

"Hi Jason." A good greeting nothing wrong with this is there?

"Pam. Isn't the weather awful?" On the surface this seems a harmless response but let's look at this objectively. What is actually happening? The weather is being criticised. Criticism is a negative act.

"Mr. Jenkins said the same thing to me yesterday, and I told him without heavy rain the sewers and gutters wouldn't get flushed, the lakes wouldn't be replenished and we would have no fresh drinking water." Pam is being polite, but has offered a positive outcome for the heavy rain.

"I didn't know you visited the Jenkins." With Pam having spoken up about her previous conversation with Mr. Jenkins the whole tone and subject matter of the conversation has improved.

"I didn't need to Mr. Jenkins was on his way into the house after his hospital visit. Between his appointments he's able to finish the models he's making for his grandchildren."

Now the information as to why Mr. Jenkins has been inside doing models is known.

No judgement issue.

Now I realise reading this you may think what planet is this woman on. No one would have a conversation like this. Really?

"Morning." Sally says as she passes Trudy on her way for morning tea.

"What's good about it? Oh and there's no milk left" says Trudy.

Often at work I overhear or am part of discussions which are negative. Is this wrong? Not necessarily but balance is important. If someone is being criticised just stop and think about something that the person does that is good. I have found that by acknowledging what a person is saying it is quite easy to remind that person about the good things the person they are talking about is doing as well. This can shift a conversation to a more positive level. In these situations we have choices for example:

You could walk away and not get caught up in it.

Make a statement that you are not going to say negative things or listen to negative things about someone

Whatever you decide to do be smart and make a conscious decision about your action.

When the frustrations of everyday life meet the frustrations within your work life.

Yes this happens. Unfortunately although the environment may alter human nature doesn't. We all have days like this from time to time. I am no exception. Do I vent? Absolutely. Does it help? In the short term it helps me. Does it help others? Probably not, but if I'm honest in the heat of the moment I am caught up in the venting.

I used to vent a lot and very often. On occasion I still do but when that happens now it is after I have exhausted all the tools in my toolkit. Once having vented though a good long walk and time to reflect usually presents an opportunity however small that gives me the starting point to resolve the issue.

I am hoping over the next five years that my venting will have ceased altogether. Why? Well like a lot of things lately I see things differently, and for what they actually are.

Living with frustration

Frustration is just that frustration usually with a person's behaviour or a situation that is not resolved.

Frustration is not the same as or to be confused with anger. Once I have identified the feeling as coming from frustration I use a strategy to deal with the frustration and this negates the need for anger, so I no longer get angry when I'm frustrated therefore I vent a lot less.

Back to the airbags. When I clambered with

help out of the car and was standing on the sidewalk I looked into the car and saw that the airbags had gone off. Until then I had no idea that the smell in the car was from the airbags and that I had inhaled the propellant from the airbags.

With my hands stinging and my fingers swelling I removed my rings, and kept asking why, are my hands, fingers, and wrists so painful?

At two o'clock in the morning when I was woken with breathing difficulties and went into the lounge to sit in my lazy boy chair to ease those difficulties I still had not made the connection to the airbags.

When I was at the hospital and the doctor examining me said it was a blessing I was wearing my seat belt and the car had airbags I was agreeing with her.

The bruising across my torso was a very dark and vibrant montage of colour, and my hands, fingers and wrists were throbbing.

Weeks later however when I was doing everything I was told to do by the doctor, not driving, not lifting things, no keyboarding, and taking prescribed medication and I was still in considerable pain where my hands, fingers and wrists were concerned I became frustrated.

Months later I did become angry though because I was told by a medical professional that my tingling hands were from Overuse Syndrome which was not true. I had no problem with my hands prior to the accident. I went back to my GP who explained what happens when an airbag is deployed in a frontal impact situation. He explained that it would be months not weeks and still more months until all that damage began to heal.

"I can't tell you exactly when but you will know because your clicking will gradually become less noticeable. Keep up the good work."

Eight months have passed. I am still clicking but not all the time and not as loudly which is extremely helpful if you are watching a thriller with others present in the room.

My anger on that occasion came from my being negated. Being negated is a very negative thing to have happen to you. Not only was I negated, my enquiry wasn't given the merit it deserved. My notes weren't read. I was looked at. I am over 50. I use a computer, the assumption was made without a physical examination of the affected area. This has now been rectified. Why? Because after I got angry I decided to get a second opinion. No matter what happens to you if you feel you haven't been taken seriously or you feel in your gut something isn't right, you are entitled to a second opinion and that is on anything.

You know we are blessed with intuition it is there to keep us safe. If you feel something is wrong or not quite right listen to that and act on it. Always, always keep yourself safe in all situations.

Have my hands got better more quickly? No. Have they got worse? No. Have I done nothing to help them? No. I have received massage on my hands which has kept them supple. Have I had surgery? No. Can I do more with my hands now? Yes. Am I pain free? No but I have much longer periods without pain. In short my expectations with the right information have been more realistic which has taken away the frustration. The reality of my situation is firmly in the forefront of my mind and even with the injuries I sustained from the impact of the airbag I am a very grateful lady indeed.

Seat belts and airbags saved our lives and saved us from more serious injuries. Common sense and patience has made my quality of life a reality. I will in time be nearly back to where I was prior to the accident. Technology has helped. I use a speech recognition programme to do my writing now and I hardly ever touch my keyboard.

My husband found me the software solution and that is another big lesson I've learned. Instead of being the one who took care of the needs of everyone else I have found someone very special who is taking care of my needs, and he has been beside me for over thirty years. Out of adversity comes hope and love. My Poppa used to tell me that when he spoke to me of his campaigns in the first and second world wars, and now I understand what he meant.

No matter what happens there is a way forward for yourself and those around you.

Chapter 2. Second chance discovery

Starting over at fifty two years of age. Yes fifty two and finding a new zest for life. A new direction.

Some have said there are not enough years left I should have made this second chance discovery at a more opportune time, which as we know is code for when you were much younger. I discount any such talk as negative and not at all relevant to me in the now.

I believe it is never too late. Never too late to learn. Never too late to discover something new. Never too late to love. Never too late for anything. If you live in the now and focus your mind clearly on what you want, believe it will be yours, you will have it. Will you have it today? That depends on what you want, will you have it tomorrow? Next month? If you want it and you believe it is yours already you will have it the timing will be right for you. Just be focused and believe and it will happen. Bit by bit, moment by moment you will get the life you see for yourself and you will enjoy every moment of it.

What is the life I want? One that gives me all that I want and not just for me to gain alone I have a plan and I see the life I want unfolding each day. I see it and already parts of that life have come to fruition.

Believe then believe some more

Never lose faith. You must believe in what you want each time you think of exactly what type of life you actually want. This is paramount.

It has taken me some time to get my head around this concept.

We are taught from a young age by people we love honour and respect to live our lives in accordance with their accepted beliefs and values. It is not until we are older that we can develop our own belief and value systems.

This will at times be frowned upon by those who have raised us or have been beside us for a long time. I need you to understand this is not a bad thing. This is quite normal.

You must realise that you are embarking on something new. Something that would quite possibly threaten even offend those who have done their very best for you up until now.

Although you may feel their resistance. Although you may be see their disapproval. Although they may offer you words of advice which is contrary to your new beliefs fear not. Step forward in full faith and knowledge that a better life awaits you and is yours for the taking. This new life will be full of riches in every aspect of your life.

I'm going to give you an example of how this can occur in everyday life.

What I have observed

Some years ago I worked with a lady we will know her as Janet. Janet had very low ability when it came to reading and numeracy. Janet was married. Her husband needed constant care. On a daily basis people would come to their home to assist her husband with his every day needs. During this time Janet got lots of advice. People expected Janet to manage without difficulty the running of the house. Until his illness Janet's husband had run the house. He had held a full-time job. In fact he had done everything for Janet. The

25

illness changed everything. One day Janet was doing menial chores, and then in a flash and in the worst possible way Janet found she was expected to do everything else as well.

One of the people a Care giver suggested to Janet that she get some help so she could manage their house better.

This is how I first met Janet. One of the things Janet needed immediate help with was the weekly shopping list. By the time Janet had come to me her shopping had been done by the use of her picture vocabulary. This meant Janet would buy things with the appropriate picture on them. Now for Janet this was a good strategy to use. It was efficient. It meant the cupboards were full. It meant food was on the table. What is the problem you may be asking? Well the problem for Janet was the grocery bill every week was more than the money allocated for food. This was happening because Janet was not able to read the labels on the food items that were cheaper to purchase. For example the budget items. These items have words on the labels, and only words. No pictures. So if you cannot read the labels you have no idea what you are buying.

One of the things we looked at first was what Janet and her husband ate every week. I have to say the menu though nutritious was lacking in variety.

Once we had established that types of meals that Janet was preparing now, and compared that to what had been done prior to her husband's illness we began to compile a list of items with both a picture and a word for the shopping glossary. Now this may seem to be a little over the top. I can assure you for Janet this made a huge difference. Janet now had a reference or shopping dictionary at her disposal in the supermarket that looked like well just a shopping list.

For Janet this was important. It didn't matter that her shopping list was pages long. It only mattered that it looked like a shopping list for people passing Janet in the supermarket aisle while she was shopping.

The very first week Janet used her new list she left the supermarket with additional choices in her trolley than she had managed previously.

That week her husband got to have his favourite dish.

As the weeks went by we worked together on looking at the flyers or junk mail that came in the post to see what specials there were that week. This helped Janet to stay within her budget. As the weeks went by Janet grew in confidence and began to shop with minimal need of her special shopping list. Just eight weeks into our program Janet had no use of her special shopping list at all. Janet would write her shopping list. Go to the supermarket. Fill her trolley and be within her budget at the checkout every week.

Now you have to see Janet as a whole person. Janet knew that she had $120 per week for food. Janet had been told she could not spend over $120 per week.

Having progressed with Janet beyond the shopping list to reading and answering other correspondence I was surprised many weeks later when Janet raised a shopping problem with me.

Janet had gone to the supermarket bought her groceries and at the checkout realised she had two dollars more to spend to make the total up to $120. So Janet bought herself a bar of chocolate and left the store. When Janet got home her husband looked at the grocery docket and asked for the additional two dollars. Janet had paid for the chocolate with the change from the $120 her groceries being $118 she had been handed two dollars change and used that independently to purchase the chocolate. With no hesitation Janet told her husband she had spent the two dollars on a bar of chocolate.

Now according to Janet this created a problem because, her husband as pleased as he was that she was keeping within the food budget did not appreciate Janet making a decision on her own to benefit her alone when she was out on her own.

What we need to acknowledge here is that the dynamic of the family had changed, and that change had brought about more change. Janet thought she was doing well and bought a bar of chocolate and managed to stay on budget. Her husband had never experienced Janet making an impromptu decision based on self-interest. What you need to realise here is that Janet's husband is not a bad person. He didn't at any stage say to Janet that she was wrong to have bought the chocolate bar. He did however acknowledge that her behaviour had changed and he wasn't sure how he felt about that. Janet had mixed feelings about this exchange.

Change

You see change never happens in isolation. When one thing changes, other things must change as well.

After the accident something within me

changed. I felt different. I wanted more. I thought about many of the people that have worked with me over the years. I really thought about them. I remembered where those people were when they first came to address their needs, and I thought about where those people are and what they are doing now. Without exception all of them are in a better place. All of them are independent.

Am I pleased for them? Of course I am. I am pleased that they embarked on a journey that led them to a better life. A better quality of life. And in some cases a better quantity of life. People who sat at home hiding who now go out and join committees, clubs, are actively involved in their families, communities and in many cases work.

As a wider community many people have benefited from the actions and the change of a few.

This power to help in our wider community is within every one of us. Once we start with ourselves we can then improve things for our families, and by extension our whole communities benefit.

Have a think about what you expect to happen in your daily life. Do you expect a stubborn colleague to be stubborn? Just because that person is generally stubborn doesn't mean you have to expect that from that person. If you expect that person to be congenial and cooperative often enough the day will come when you will either be working alongside a congenial cooperative person or they may be transferred out or leave and go somewhere else.

If you expect to be late chances are you will be late. If you expect to arrive with time to spare then you will arrive with time to spare.

Expectations come from thoughts.

If you think negatively about things, negative things happen or continue to happen.

Understanding how you think in relation to your expectations is crucial to you effecting positive change in your life.

Expectations are extremely important in this change. If we expect more and believe we will receive more, our expectations upon receipt will also change. We will begin to expect more and more will come.

I was standing at a pedestrian crossing on a very wet and windy day when a car stopped to let me cross. I mouthed "thank you" and received a barrage of abuse. It wasn't until later that I realised my thank you could easily have been mistaken for another commonly used phrase which also ends in ....you.

I held no animosity to the people who were verbally abusing me. At the time I was pleased to have crossed the road and gotten under cover on the other side out of the wind and rain, and being able to continue on with my errands.

What did this teach me? Did I learn not to say thank you? Of course not I learned that people are not used to being thanked. People are used to being abused and subconsciously they expect that so they react in a similar fashion themselves.

Can you see how our immediate world, the space we share with others can be unpleasant at times. We are the ones who need to change that and we can. Every day we can do something to change that. No matter where you live. No matter who you are around at home, at work, at school, in groups, in churches, sports clubs, you can make your life a lot more pleasant by being pleasant to people, by loving people, by not being afraid to let the love spill over to others.

If you are reading this and thinking that won't happen with my group, friends, or family then you need to keep reading.

Start with a smile, a smile first thing in the morning followed by the words "Good morning" said with enthusiasm, followed by "I am so looking forward to today" and when you are asked why simply answer "today is my starting over day. Something great is going to happen for me today," then get on and enjoy the day. Do the best you can do that day. If people are talking about others and saying unkind things you can add a positive about that person then leave.

You will feel different inside and you will want more of that feeling, that is the feeling that will help you expect more and want more and be ready for more.

We are not meant to be inhabiting this planet in this body to be miserable, unhappy, or broke, our purpose here is to do good, be good, and receive in abundance lots of good things.

If we are good to others, by helping them, be supportive of them, encourage them, love them, and praise them, we will get all that back and more, so the more people we can help, support, love and praise the more we will get back.

This is not meant to be a chore. This will come naturally once you are able to see life in a more positive way.

So how do we do this?

Be honest with yourself. I mean really honest. You need to let go of all the things that are negative in your life like bad feelings, jealousy, hurt, anger. With these things in your life you are holding yourself back from all the good things that are waiting for you.

Recently an advertised position came up which I decided not to apply for because of what was written in the advertisement. Later I found out that the job advertised wasn't the position at all and by that time the position had been filled. At the time I felt angry because had I had all the information I would have applied for the role, but that opportunity has now gone. Am I cross with the person who got the position? No I wish her well and am doing all I can to help her. There is one aspect of the job I would love but many other aspects that I would if I am honest find boring.

If that position came up again and was advertised properly would I apply for it? Absolutely because I can deal with the boring bits to do the bit of the job I love. In the mean time I am grateful for the job I have now I love it. I get to help people most days. I get to laugh a lot. I get to learn a lot and I have definite expectations now that I didn't have then.

What I have learned is that opportunities still come to you if you have definite expectations.

I see the life I want now and everyday little by little my life is getting better. Not just a little better a lot better.

We have another wedding anniversary coming up soon and I am reminded of a card I saw last year where the person had sent a card to her husband of 45 years saying "Stay with me the best is yet to come."

That sums it up for me. No matter what has happened to date the best is yet to come I say bring it on and on and on.

We increasingly find ourselves in this day and age being bombarded by images of the world. In years gone by there was the paper and probably only the paper for some people. The images would have been sketched and they were minimal in terms of content in the paper. Most people couldn't read so the paper was small in distribution number and by location. As education spread and became mandatory more people were able to read. The papers were then in more demand and there were more than one or two daily papers so competition came into play. Pictures backed up a headline and pictures also told a story. Sketches were replaced with photos. The next step in the evolution of news came with the invention of the radio. Each radio station had a news segment.

Radio with pictures was next and each movie theatre had a newsreel that would play before the scheduled movie started. This proved to be an effective and mobilising tool for Britain, America, Germany and other countries in the Second World War.

Television became the next stage and news was beamed directly into homes. Papers were still popular but television was starting to find its feet. Documentary programmes looked at news in a more in depth way. Pictures with real people talking, gripping and profitable stuff.

Today we have the internet. The internet is full of images with words around them. We are literally bombarded with information but information is NOT knowledge. Information is just that, information. Information can be used as a tool to get a result for someone or something. Whether that be a cause, a person needing help, a truth to be told, a political viewpoint to be exploited, a lifestyle choice to be normalised these are the realities of the common age. The age we are all living in.

This in my view can become a barrier to our growth as people. Why? Simply because it is so easy to get caught up in all the information that we can lose sight of who we are, and where we want to be.

Guilt

Guilt is a negative emotion that is quite frankly a good merchandising skill. I will give you an example. You can be inundated with images of people who are facing dreadful situations such as flood, famine, disease and a caption along the lines of "for the price of one cup of coffee a day". This works on people for several reasons but one of those reasons is because it makes people feel guilty about their one cup of coffee a day.

Do I buy one cup of coffee a day? No, but if I did I would enjoy it and I wouldn't feel guilty about it. Sadly I believe I am in the minority. Do I give to those in need absolutely, but I give because I want to not because I am ' guilted ' into it. I am happy to give and the more I give the happier I am to do so.

We have a growing trend in the western world to do things using a competitive model. This model also is present in our fundraising arena.

Yes there are huge problems in the world. Yes we need to do something. Yes great works are being done. Yes there are huge charitable organisations that are doing what they can to help so what's the problem?

If we all just got on with giving a little without the machine that costs to make or compel us to do so we would actually donate more with less cost and greater benefit to many more.

Now I am not just talking about money here. I give help to those who have literacy and numeracy needs. I concentrate on delivering the basics. Why just the basics? Basics are the foundation we can build on to find and know success. Without the basics in anything we cannot meet our full potential we are always reliant on someone else.

There is nothing like the buzz I get when I see someone I have worked with over a period of time achieve success on their own. I mean there is nothing more gratifying. I know that person is making a positive difference to everyone in their life and more good flows from that than anything.

Never underestimate what an individual can do. What one person can do? What you can do.

Start today. Start by looking and honestly

evaluating how YOU see the world. Do you see the world as a place where other people are happy? Other people get to have what they want? Do you judge people who have plenty? Do you say things like when is enough, enough? Why should they have more? They have plenty or more than enough already.

If you are thinking like this you are not allowing yourself the time to focus on what you want. If you do not know what you want how are you ever going to receive it?

You see people who have plenty are people who know what they want. If they are born into a family with plenty they themselves have no problem with expecting more and feeling good about having more.

For some people who feel guilty about all they have they subsequently lose it all. Why is that? Bad luck? No. More than likely they don't want it, don't respect what they have or what they have does not make them happy. I know many people who have not a lot of financial or material wealth but they are rich successful people. When I talk to them about it they all without exception say similar things like I am so happy with my family, or I have the job I want, or I have grown my business to where I want it to be. These people know what they want.

Do you? Do you really?

No matter how out there something is or seems to be, if you want it and you believe it will be for you and come to fruition for you, act like you have it already and see what happens.

Chapter 3. Free will

We are told we are born with free will. Along the way life comes in, and little by little our freedoms are absorbed into the daily grind of life. It is the same for all of us. We can be free again. Take ownership of your thoughts. Have good thoughts reap good rewards. My grandmother used to say to me (and she was a true lady) she was always happy. She helped others and she was happy. She cooked and she was happy. She visited with her sister, who was married into a family of great wealth and she was happy to spend time with her sister. Never jealous or envious. Both sisters immigrated to New Zealand from Scotland when they were young women but their paths were quite different. I learned from my grandmother that if you see the best in life and be the best you can be you will have a blessed life. I see that now more than ever. The older I get the more I see it, live it and believe it. I also know now that if I want more that's okay and I can have more. I have a veracious appetite for more of some things so I can help more, grow more, be more beneficial to this world, but I am unable to be those things if I don't look after myself first and I am learning how to do that. That is the biggest thing of all. We are raised to provide for others, help others, be there for others and I have no problem with that. I have been doing that my whole life, but as I said near the beginning of this book I had an event occur which has made me look at things differently and see things differently.

By putting myself first does that mean I no longer care for my family? No. No longer help others? No. If you can take one thing from this book I hope it is the knowledge that by taking care of yourself first you can do more, for yourself and for others. Taking care of yourself first is not being selfish. Being selfish is acting in a way that means you are self centred and that all you do is for self-gain. Putting yourself first and taking care of yourself is giving you what you need. A sense of value of yourself. Value as to why you are here. Taking care of yourself means you are able to perform better for yourself and others. It is the difference between falling asleep in a movie and seeing and enjoying the whole movie. It will enable you to enjoy even the smallest things which you would normally miss. An in depth conversation with someone instead of a superficial one, or the perfunctory nod and acknowledgement. You know sometimes when we stop for a chat it is us who gets the benefit as well as the other person. Slow down start enjoying the little things and better things come to you.

Start today. Start with a smile and or a kind word.

How often do people say to you "I know you are busy" Are you really busy or are you too rushed to be busy with the things that matter? We are spiritual, emotional beings and we need to connect with people.

If electricity has a circuit disrupted what happens? No power. Lots of inconvenience, frustration, plans put on hold, opportunities missed in some cases.

We are like that to. If we do not connect properly with others we create frustration, inconvenience and worse, we allow the other person to feel they are not worthy of our time. What we are saying by our actions is my time is more valuable than yours. Now how arrogant is that? Take time to think, really think about what your actions are saying. Be totally honest. If you were treated like this would you like it? If the answer to the last question is no then change your actions.

Changing actions doesn't need to be a chore. It doesn't need to be hard. Not all of your actions need to be changed.

Quite often if you change one behaviour other behaviours change for the better by default.

Frowning is an easy one to look at. If you are prone to frowning you will feel flat or negative a lot of the time. If you change that frown to a smile you will feel uplifted, happy and be exercising your facial muscles in a positive way that your wrinkles will approve of both now and in later life. Where do you think the term laughter lines comes from! If you look at laughter lines they go out and slightly up enhancing the cheek bones, and the eye line.

Frown lines make for a furrowed brow. A closed look and pinched look around the eyes. No amount of make-up can change the direction of your lines or the story they are telling.

Start the day with a smile. In the morning close your eyes and smile for at least one

minute. Do that for a week and feel the
difference.

Ideas

Ideas are great. Never be afraid of having an
idea. Never be afraid to research the viability
of an idea.

We get ideas for a reason. Ideas give us the
opportunity to change our circumstances
potentially.

I say potentially because not all ideas may
come to fruition. Is this a bad thing?
Absolutely not. Ideas form the basis of change
but to be effective you have to look into them,
have a plan to go with them and then
implement them.

To do the implementation part of the process
you have to see the plan for your idea in
action. I will give you a simple example.

Sam had an idea to hold a fundraiser to
support his friend Ted who needed money to
compete in his sport overseas.

Sam looked into what made money quickly
and a work mate of his suggested that a
biscuit or cookie bake would be successful.

Sam got a group of friends to put in for the
ingredients as their contribution for Ted and

then he approached a woman who did baking for the annual school fundraiser and asked her to help. This lady suggested that people get order forms so the goods were pre-ordered. The order went out through a network of people and when they were filled the baker mobilized a team of bakers. The fundraiser was a success and Ted was very grateful for the financial assistance he received. The benefit of this idea wasn't just confined to Ted however. The community as a whole benefited. They were mentioned in the newspaper articles about Ted. They were all involved and had a pot luck dinner the evening Ted was to race so they could watch his event together.

None of this would have happened if Sam hadn't had an idea. An idea that responded to a need. An idea that was researched. An idea that had a plan. An idea that was implemented with the plan into action. An idea that met the need and was successful.

Many people are often involved in an idea coming to fruition so having positive people in your life does help to pull ideas and plans off. How do we have positive people in our lives? We ask for them and we are positive around people. If you are asked to do something try saying yes from time to time and see what great things come into your life as a result.

Say yes with a smile and it will be worthwhile.
Say yes with a heavy heart and it will be just
another chore.

Work ethic

There are three types of work in my history;
the paid kind, the unpaid kind and the
voluntary kind.

The paid kind is when you do a job and get
paid for it with money by way of a wage or
salary.

The unpaid kind when you are sent off to do
work with no pay for the actual work done.
This is often called work experience and when
you are older you often have the experience
and work for someone who does not have to
pay you.

The voluntary kind is where you volunteer
your services or expertise to someone or a
cause that needs something done with no
expectation of being paid.

What all these things have in common is
work. Work is work. Make no mistake if you
are doing something for someone you are
working the means by which that may or may
not be rewarded is irrelevant to the work done.
If you are doing work for someone or
something do the best job you can regardless

of whether you are being given money for it.

All work is valued and for each job you do you are adding value to your community no amount of money will compensate for a great work ethic. Give your children and grandchildren jobs to do. You can give pocket money or treats as a reward for some of the jobs done but let them learn that all jobs are to be done well even if only some of them are paid for with money or treats. A good focus is on the quality of the job done and giving lots of praise. Praise is worth a lot more growing good work ethic than money. Money can be spent and it's gone. Praise on the other hand can be recalled and give a feeling of worth to the recipient. A thirteen year old said to his father: "I remember when I helped Poppy wash the car he said I did a good job, and took me to the model railway for a train ride." The father replied "but you were only four." The son asked "Was I?"

We need to praise more. We need to appreciate more. We need to love more. We need to thank more. Money cannot supply any of these important things.

Giving

Here it comes you may be thinking "the more you give the more you receive issue," and you would be right, but only from my personal experience.

I recently overheard a discussion by two people at a conference about tithing and they had opposing views. Tithing is about giving ten percent of what you have to others. The general reason for this is to help those in need. Tithing is a biblical principle and many churches have relied on tithing to get their good works done. This conversation got me thinking about how much of a weekly pay I was giving to those in need and I was shocked to realise that it added up to more than ten percent. It also made me look at what I was giving money to, for example many raffles are for sale in our community to raise funds for sports, trips, community groups and they are between two and five dollars a ticket. It's just one ticket here and one ticket there but in a month they can add up. Do I begrudge helping a team or individual reach a goal they have set? No. Do I expect a big pat on the back? No. Do I expect to win every raffle I buy? No. So why do I do it? I buy the ticket because I know that without my help someone who cannot afford the experience will miss out.

Where we live we have a community vegetable scheme. This is where a community purchases large volumes of vegetables at a reduced rate and grows their own vegetables then sells these on to families for a set fee per week. This scheme has helped hundreds of families in our area. I belong to this scheme because I believe the more people who support the scheme the more sustainable the scheme is. One of the bonuses of belonging to this scheme is that we cannot eat all the vegetables every week so a portion of our bag is donated to someone who can. Never be afraid to share when there is an excess. I always look in the bag and work out what I have enough of at home already and give the fresh produce to the recipient with our blessing.

Small acts like this soon add up to ten percent per week. The ten percent is not just about money. Some people I know put ten percent aside each week and if they hear of someone in need anonymously donate to those in need. They may not necessarily give them the money but a bag of groceries or some meat may be purchased and dropped off for those people. It is all giving.

What is interesting to me is the way people seem to focus all their attention on the ten percent they have to give and never the ninety percent they are able to keep.

When you focus on the ninety percent you will

see you have more than enough so putting aside ten percent is a privilege.

As I said earlier never feel pressured into doing or giving anything. If you can't give freely and with a loving heart you are merely handing over and that is NOT giving. What makes giving so special is the love that's attached to it.

"The more you give the more you receive" happens when you add the love to the action.

If you are not doing it I would encourage you to give it a try. If you are giving like me you may find out you are actually giving more than the ten percent required and there's nothing wrong with that.

If you find you are not in a position some weeks to give ten percent in monetary aid look at all the skills you give to others. Giving is giving and provides aid in all forms to those in need. Give with love and see the difference you can make to those in need. Giving is powerful.

Chapter 4. Changing your channel

Scenario 1:

It's early in the evening all your chores are done and you turn the television on. You sit back in your chair to be entertained and find that what you are watching is not the right thing for you. Do you stay tuned? Switch channels? Turn the television off?

Scenario 2:

It's early in the evening the dishes are done and people in your house are watching television. There is a programme you would like to watch but others are already watching a programme that interests them. Do you ask them to change the channel? Do you stay and watch what they are watching? Do you leave the room?

At times the situations we find ourselves in can seem either déjà vu, not worth staying for or of benefit to someone else.

When you find yourself in this situation what can you do? You can stay and get stuck in a rerun of a very bad movie. You can change your environment by moving to another room, situation, or house. Go for a walk and change your immediate environment until things improve. You can turn your head on and drown out all the other noise. Turn your volume up what do you hear? What is your inner voice saying to you?

If you are in a situation that is not good for you, you can leave it or change it? You can ask for help. Make a plan and work towards it. You CAN do something about your situation, your life, your environment. Be encouraged. Will it be hard? Maybe. Will it be costly? Maybe? Will I be better off? Time will tell. Is it worth doing? Absolutely.

Why? Sometimes when we decide to make a change that is all we need to do to enable ourselves to see things differently, to help us reconnect with "me" and that in itself is enough. Other times we need to get help or information and put things in place before we can actually make the change and to start with the change may not seem to be what we thought it might be. The benefits we expect may not materialise straight away. We may be physically removed from our former situation but our mind is still back there. That is why I said "time will tell". In general though if you turn the television off and leave the room you will enjoy the time you spend somewhere else. Why wouldn't you? The television programme wasn't giving you what you needed.

If you are in a situation or environment that is not giving you what you need be proactive and do something to change it. You may not need to physically leave but you may need to leave what you are doing and try something else within your environment to get your needs met. There is nothing wrong with that.

Communication

Recently in a large city in our country the remains of a dead man were found. He had been dead several months.

He lived in a council apartment surrounded by apartments and people and no one realised he wasn't around. He continued to receive his benefit. His rent and power were paid. To all intents and purposes he was still very much with us. Alive and well.

How can this have happened?

With the advent of the technological era this is happening more and more. We can do our banking online, pay our bills online, purchase our food online. In short we can set things up to be done automatically and so long as money comes in also automatically money goes out.

I go into workplaces where policy and procedure manuals are a mandatory requirement for a business to have. So long as a business has them they pass their audit. Many businesses have what appears to be an up to date policy and procedure manual because the date on the first few pages has been updated to that year but on inspection there may well be things in those manuals that are completely out of date or irrelevant for the current working environment.

How can we address these things?

Quite simply by putting people back into the system. We have depersonalised many things.

We are thinking, feeling, beings and we need to be seen and heard. We need to talk to one another. Not txt one another when we are in the same room. No actually talk, engage, converse.

In a workplace if your policy and procedure manuals are annually updated ask your boss if you can have input into that process. Get a group of people together and look at the manuals and see if they are practical for what you are doing.

Earlier this year I went to an Industry Training Conference and we had a speaker who decided that in order to get her staff to take on training she would do the training as well. What this highlighted for her was that the manuals the staff had been saying were of no help to them in their jobs was actually true so a complete rewrite was done. Why were they no help to staff? They weren't written by the people who did the jobs. Why did they pass the audit process? Very possibly because they looked right.

When things look right that's not always okay, but when things are right everyone benefits.

Having systems in place is not the same as having accurate information.

Having information is not the same as being knowledgeable.

The information said the tenant was paying rent.

The workplace had passed its audit.

Two very different and apparently unrelated things.

The knowledge however was very different.

The tenant had died.

The workplace had inappropriate manuals.

When you don't see someone for a while ask around and see if someone knows what they may be up to.

When someone tells you something stop and listen.

We don't have to live in someone's pocket to make a difference. We don't have to bring the same subject up over and over again to be heard, but if we take an interest and act on it, it can make all the difference.

The economics we live with

We live in a world of fiscal dominance. We have stock units, labour units, stock markets, labour markets. Boom times and recessions. All these trends actually affect people.

Put people into the equation. Communicate with people. You may be surprised by what people know. We don't all see things the same way.

I was recently at a presentation on how technology is sold to education providers. There are lots of presentations done about new software packages. Marketing to a target audience in other words which is great if you are selling a product. Unfortunately many of these products do not deliver on the hype that they promote.

Nothing can replace teaching. Value added aids are great and there is a valid place for those, but knowledge is something that is learned, you cannot copy and paste it.

I have worked with people who once they have filled in gaps, or learned something new and have the basics sorted achieve great things across the wide spectrum of their lives. They can only do this because they have the basics. Because they have knowledge. On base knowledge you can build amazing things. If you know someone or are someone who struggles with learning you can do something about it.

Go to adult classes and find out what it is you haven't learned yet and learn it. Will it take too long? If it takes two years or five years out of a lifetime and gives you the life you want. It's one of the best investments you will ever make. I encourage you to make a deposit today.

Labels

People often say they are too old to do this and too old to do that. I am fifty two as I write this and many people talk to me as if I am already in the golden years. This could in part be because my hairdresser has been ill and I am not as pristine as usual in the hair department, but it is more likely to be that younger people under forty five have this thing about age. Once you are past fifty you are on your way to retirement so redundant. Now this may be untrue of many but it is definitely true of some.

I am starting over and there are things I want to achieve before I am eighty years of age. I don't need another label slapped on me I have had many over the years not one of them has actually enhanced me as an individual not one. They may have been correct to the situation or circumstance but they had nothing to do with me personally.

We are not products for sale, DVD's or books in a library to be categorised for a catalogue. We are to all intents and purposes people who have a role to play on this earth. Do I know what mine is? Not exactly but I do know what I want to do and how by achieving that I can add value to others. This is not an age related condition. Be definite and know what you want then see yourself doing it. Do I know how I am going to achieve it? Not yet but then I didn't know how I was going to be as a parent until I started raising children. I didn't know how I would be as an adult student when I went back to school at thirty two years of age, but I went every day I had classes, attended my classes, passed and received adult student of the year. I turned up and applied myself and with those two ingredients success is going to happen. We don't have to know how, we just need to start doing.

A few years ago when I was doing some radio script writing I had a school friend who asked "Did you ever believe your words would be reaching people in Central America?"

I said "No but I knew my words would reach someone I wouldn't have done a writing diploma if I didn't want people to read or hear my words." Now you may say that I was being cold, but I can assure you the tone with which I said these words wasn't in the least bit cold.

I did a writing diploma so I could write better. I wanted to write better so people could read what I had written. The advent of the radio writing came about by divine intervention and I never second guessed that opportunity for one second. I was asked to do it. I sent a script off for them to look at they said okay

and I began writing for them. Honestly it was
the best job I've ever had. I love to write yes
but I had prepared myself to write across
different forums by doing my writing diploma.
I had also believed I would be a writer. Is that
my purpose for being? I don't know but while
I am here I intend to do the things I love
doing. I love writing so it's a no brainer really.

Do I only write? No writing hasn't paid the
bills yet but within my paying job I write. I
write to communicate with others. I write to
help others meet their requirements in the
education field. I write to inform in a
simplified way. I write instructional material
in specialised language for a targeted audience
that has become part of my job.

When I am at home writing however that is
completely different. I am not constrained
and it doesn't feel like work.

Do you have something you like to do that
doesn't feel like work? Can you turn it into
work? Can you do more of it? Do you get
feelings of satisfaction when you have done it?
If so keep doing it. We do not have to get paid
for everything we love to do, but we do need to
do what we are passionate about.

I don't have time you may be thinking. If you
are passionate about something or you want

to learn about something or do something that you have an interest in I would encourage you to do it. It really is good for our well-being. Personal satisfaction and fulfillment is good for the soul.

If you love kids and yours have grown up and left home volunteer at a school or do a qualification in early childhood education, or pediatric nursing it is never too late to do something you want to do and only you know what that is. If you don't have the financial means find another way to meet your need.

Once you do you will find you enjoy getting up every day and you will start every day with a smile. You won't have to consciously smile you will just be smiling.

Chapter 5. Work ethic

Many times I will hear employers say "Where is the work ethic these days?" The reality is you don't learn work ethic at work.

From what I have seen across my lifetime to date is work ethic in action starts from an extremely young age. The "pick up your toys and put them in your toy box" stage and continues to be developed with consistency over many years.

Consistency is the key here. The more consistency the better the work ethic. No one is ever too old to learn how apply themselves in an environment to get a job done but work ethic is a different thing to that.

Initiative and independent action is also a big

part of work ethic. If you have finished your work for the day, and you have some time left to work, a person with a good work ethic will either offer to do something for someone else or do a job that needs doing because they have some time so they just do it. A person without a good work ethic will go to a computer and play a game or spend time on the internet gaining information for their own benefit.

This can cause huge problems in families, workplaces and communities. Why?

One of the major problems is a disparity of treatment. Those with good work ethic are often expected to do more than those who don't display a good work ethic. Like most things, work ethic is a learned behaviour and it is never too late to learn it. If you are carrying people in your home, workplace or community group start talking about how sharing the load is beneficial for everyone and expect people around you to help share the workload. Speak up, model what is required, engage people and get them to help you. Mumbling or grizzling to others about this is counter- productive and negative. Be a positive role model and let people know what is expected and expect them to comply. Will there be some reluctance, some resistance? Initially there may, but be consistent and everyone will benefit. It is not all right for people to get by on the good will or good works of others. We all need to contribute. To do our bit, and that includes emptying the office rubbish bin from time to time. If we put rubbish in why shouldn't we empty it out?

The blue days

I thought you said we mustn't be negative? If that is what you are thinking or saying out loud I would have to answer yes I have said just that.

Blue days don't need to be negative. A blue day can be an opportunity to do something completely different. Read a book. Leave a chore and go for a walk. Phone a friend. Anything you can do on a blue day that stops you feeling blue is a positive. What helps me on a blue day is thinking of good things other people do.

If you find you are having lots of blue days seek medical help.

Thoughts

I don't know about you but I get so busy during the day I have to remind myself to have positive thoughts. Sometimes positive thoughts just arrive (usually after someone has done something good or helpful or something good has happened or arrived), other times I have to stop and think about positive things.

Negative thoughts on the other hand seem to arrive with monotonous regularity and at the most inconvenient times. They can be like a tape running through your head once something has triggered them. It could be dropping a pen at work then the thought "what else am I going to drop" pops in and before you know it the piece of papers next to the pen slides onto the floor as well.

As soon as I get a negative thought now I close my eyes and consciously think of something positive before resuming my next task.

In 2005 I had the pleasure to work with a lady who said something that impacted on my life in a very positive way. "If you want to change the outcome change your behaviour." This wasn't directed at me, never the less I have taken it on board.

Have a good look at your situation. Are you happy, content, satisfied, safe, fulfilled where you are right now? If you have answered yes to at least three of the above I am happy for you if not guess what you may need to do "If you want to change your outcome change your behaviour."

For many years I accepted being in fifth place in my family. Why wouldn't I? Growing up I had been in fourth place shunted down the pecking order for years. I was the wrong shape for a start and that created a lifelong fear of eating. Those days are gone now because I changed my behaviour and got a better outcome. I am healthier and enjoy food. Am I a size ten? No but I now know that I can eat whatever I want and be happy about it, my body is coming back to my perfect weight for me.

Now there may be people who think I was never in fifth place and they may be correct to think that but they weren't there.

What I think is important to remember is that you are the one who is affected most by what happens to and around you. You are the one who can take a stand. You are the one who can give in for peace and allow people to run roughshod over you. You have a choice. I had a choice but I didn't have the confidence or where with all to make it, or act on it.

I am no longer in that space and for me that is a good thing, for others though it has been a rather interesting journey.

Some years ago my husband and I went into a dress shop together. I saw a crushed velvet jacket on the sale rack. I picked it up and tried it on and put it back. We looked at some other items in the shop and on our way to the door I passed the sales rack again. I picked up the jacket took it to the counter and announced "I'm having that." My husband stopped in his tracks and said, "That's not like you. What's happening?" The sales lady made herself busy putting the jacket in the bag and I got my purse out. My husband had just moments before encouraged me to buy the jacket. What happened? I did something about what I wanted and it felt great. What surprised me was that I felt as good about doing something for myself as I did about doing something for someone else. A very warm fuzzy feeling.

Obligation

It's a very murky subject obligation. The first question to be looked at is whose obligation? Followed closely by to whom? Or to what?

So let's look at some options.

The too whom is usually a parent, older sibling, employer, supervisor, or board someone deemed to be above you or someone you are in a partnership with, spouse, children, colleagues.

The too what could be in the context of a role

you have, or a charter such as a code of conduct, an agreement or moral responsibility.

In national elections held recently in this country the media had a very big part to play in the outcome of the election. Their coverage was bias for months. Bias towards the sitting government.

The government used an international event to shorten the election time that is normally given in our country for people to make up their minds.

There was a feeling amongst many people that the election was a done deal so why even bother voting.

Now I am no political commentator by any means, but in my role I heard over and over that people didn't see the need to vote. With a referendum being held at the same time as the elections there was some confusion as to what to vote for, and where to look for information on forms and things.

The referendum wording was confusing. There were two boxes one asking did you want the current system to remain.

Then underneath that a question asking if you the system was to change what system would you want? With those systems listed.

Many people for whatever reason feel disenfranchised from the system so don't vote. Traditionally in our country when that happens the sitting government remains in power.

Our country was the first in the world to give women the vote so how have we in a hundred years got to the point where a significant number of people don't feel their vote counts?

If media and we live in a world where media is delivered through different mediums, being able to manipulate a result thereby creating news rather than reporting it, which seems to be a worldwide trend at present, to whom are they the media obligated? The public? Their corporate owners?

This question has been asked earlier in this book.

Who are you obligated to? Have a good think about it.

I have spent many years of my life living under obligation to others, and I have realised that actually the person I am obligated to is myself. From that knowledge all else falls into place. If I do what is right for me, with love, honesty, integrity and intention everything else I do gives a positive result for others.

If getting a good result for others in work is right for me then the business I work for gets a good employee with a good work ethic, and in my role my clients get the attention they need and the service they need to exact a good result for them, and the business they work for. Is this a win? This is actually how it should be. This is not a selfish route in my mind, this is the route to self- fulfillment and from that only good will come. It also takes work and commitment on my part, but anything in life worth having will take that. Good intentions helps the process along.

Intentions

Let's have a brief look at intentions. What are they? 'Acts of intensifying', according to the Concise Dictionary.

What this means is that what we think about we can bring about. If we wake up thinking "I feel stuffed before I've started" you probably will feel stuffed for a good portion of your morning until you think of something else.

Many of us feel this way it is not unusual, however if you think before you go to sleep that you will wake well rested and feeling restored or full of energy you will. Skeptical?

So was I until I tried it. I tried this for one whole week and I was waking feeling better than I had in years so I keep doing it who wouldn't? I also add things to the list. In my working life when I am delivering training I intend that the training is successful and that it goes smoothly. I can tell you this is a far better platform to delivering from than expecting people to cause interruptions and hassles.

What happens in the first instance is you put a good vibe out there and when we do that we tend to relax and allow better things to happen, like a good night's sleep. I hear the pharmaceutical companies groaning at this.

Don't be afraid to have positive intentions. Don't be afraid to extend your thoughts so you benefit from the results. You deserve it.

Today

Do you remember fairy tales? They usually start with once upon a time don't they? Well I have started my life story each day with "Today I will........." and tell the world, or the empty bedroom just what I want to have happen that day. When I go to bed I am thankful for all the things that well that day and intend what will happen the next and so the pattern repeats itself.

"Once upon a time" is great for fairy tales, but I have dreams to fulfill and they happen on a daily basis. Take today for example. My husband bought me a Dictaphone so I could do my writing without having to use the keyboard or mouse. The Dictaphone is compatible with a Speech Recognition programme he also bought me. When my hands were so affected by the accident I didn't think I would be able to write again. Every day I sit and write a bit more one of my dreams is being realised. Dreams can be big or small. I have absolutely huge dreams that will be fulfilled. How do I know? Because each day my small ones are being realised, and if small ones can be realised on a daily basis, huge ones can be too.

Take this book. I chip away at it a chapter or two at a time. My dream is to write the book. My big dream is to get a publisher who will publish it. My bigger dream with regard to writing this book is to have it selling successfully internationally. But the huge dream I have for this book is that it helps people to see that they too can realise their own dreams. Improve their own quality of life. Enjoy that success and set about having many more successes. Remember when you succeed those around you benefit as well.

Nothing and I mean nothing breeds success

like achievement. One small achievement will spark a succession of success. Have a plan, works towards it, change things if you need to as you go, tweaking is okay and you will achieve. Achieving is success. Enjoy it. Be bold and try to achieve something else. It can become an addictive habit. Look around at what other things become available to you in your life as a result of achievement and success.

Chapter 6: Know your limits

A short time ago a colleague of mine was by
her own admission heading for a breakdown.
She needed to make a change. A big change
and she took the bull by the horns so to speak
and did just that. Put the wheels in motion to
make a change for herself. Two weeks after
that she met someone and is now enjoying a
positive sharing experience with a new person
in her life.

Saying no

There are times when we need to say no. How
does one do that regardless of the pressure
being applied to exact a YES?

The same way we do everything else with
honesty and integrity. If you are being asked

for money and you don't have extra money available to you at that time then the right answer for you is NO at that time. This is not being 'heartless' or 'mean' or 'mean spirited' or 'selfish' or any other such thing. If you do not have it at the time you cannot give it.

This can apply to anything time, money, committing to something in the future. For you to do justice to the situation you have to be in a position to handle it comfortably yourself. Think about that for a moment.

Let's say you have been saving for a trip or a newer car or repairs on the house and someone needs some financial help. They come to you because they know you have money put aside for something. That money is what you have saved for something you need. It is earmarked money. It is not extra money is it? Let's get clear about what extra is. Extra is what you have available over and above what you need.

If you have free time on a Tuesday afternoon and you are asked to volunteer a few hours a week then you could do that on your free time on a Tuesday afternoon if you chose to because Tuesday afternoon is extra time available in your week.

This is no different when it comes to money.

If you have money outside of your budget then is extra and you can do what you want with it.

I used to think that I was doing the right thing by helping people family mostly out by using the money I had put aside but in actuality I should have put that money in the budget because what happened was the more I helped them the further behind my repairs and maintenance got. People I had helped would have a holiday and we would not because the money I had put aside had gone to help others. Helping others is great but not when it is done to the detriment of yourself.

This lesson was brought home to me by a flyaway comment made by someone who had been helped by a family member that comment was "why would I pay interest on something when I can get people to bail me out for nicks."

We are not helping ourselves by doing right by others at the expense of ourselves. Sometimes helping others is to say NO.

Topsy Turvy

You are going along just fine. Your bills are being paid. Things are going well at home or at work or in both places. Wider things like your extended family, church life sports team, or drama club whatever it may be are ticking along and you start to get complacent. It is all happening the way you want it to right and you can sit back and just enjoy the ride?

When we are sitting back enjoying the ride and maybe taking in the scenery along the way we become complacent and when that happens yep meet my friend and soon to be yours Topsy Turvy. Topsy Turvy shows up to keep us engaged. Keep us awake. Keep us on our toes and Topsy Turvy has a very annoying habit of always without exception turning things upside down or on their head.

Something unexpected will happen. A phone call "Have you been talking to your mum today? I have just seen her and she doesn't look good." So off you go to Mum and find that she is not good. When was the last time you had good thoughts about your mum? She was fine a couple of weeks ago right? This is where we need to be vigilant. Yes we can enjoy the good things that happen for us and to us but just expecting a free ride? Nothing is free and our thoughts are no different. The cost to us is the knowledge and application daily that our thoughts must be on the right wave length. They must be good. They must be positive. They must be sincere. Even the pretend or make believe ones. We must see what is in our thoughts.

I see my dream house, playing in the pool with the grandchildren, watching our family splashing about and laughing. I see the remote control cars being raced on the tennis court. I see my new vehicle sitting next to the same model but a different colour from my husband's sitting side by side in the garage. I walk the races on my beef block dictating my next book. I see these images daily and several times a day, and I am so, so happy in these images.

The more you imagine the good for you and you enjoying the good and sharing it with others the sooner you are actually living it. I believe that with my whole heart.

I believe that without any doubt and it is happening. All the little steps that need to happen for the big picture to be properly set in the frame are happening so I am more resolved than ever to continue taking time out every day to see my life unfold the way I want and need it to for me.

Set backs

You have done everything as you should. You are well prepared. You have planned for a special event or happening and then you get the rejection letter, or are let down by someone else in the chain and you cannot go ahead with what you thought you would be doing. Why does this happen? Does it make you angry or grateful?

I recently suffered a knockback. Was I disappointed? Yes. Was I angry? No but then I wasn't on top of the world either I chose to take the view that there was something better out there for me instead.

This temporarily took the heat out of the situation at least, but as the reality of the knockback and its consequences sank in I became quite flat for a brief period of time, then kept myself busy with something I liked to do, and carried on with my day.

Just because we get a knockback this doesn't mean it is a bad thing for us. Sometimes it a lucky escape or allows us to explore a new opportunity, and sometimes knockbacks happen to people so that other people learn a lesson. Remember there is always a consequence to every situation but that doesn't mean you are responsible for the set back or the one intended to feel the consequence.

Quite often decisions made in good faith can result in the wrong people being affected negatively. No one deserves set-backs but sometimes what appears to be a set-back is actually a reset and can help you in the longer term.

How often have you heard people say something like this: "You know if I had got that job I wouldn't have met...." or "If I had been offered that position I would've been out of a job altogether. Look what happened just a few months into the contract. I was lucky."

If you have a set-back take a positive view of it and reset your thinking looking for a new opportunity. Never give up. Never give up. Always keep looking for opportunities and making the most of them. Oh yes and even when you have a set-back. Never give up. If you have been told you can do something by someone else you are capable of doing that and more. Never give up and never stop looking for a new opportunity to help you become the person or do the things you really want to do.

Chapter 7. Turning things around

You are on a path to somewhere but it is not going quite where you thought or planned it would. This happens often in our lives. Many times we are well advanced on the road before we see it is not going where we need it to for us. Quite often it has been re-routed to satisfy or meet the needs of others at our expense. What can we do?

Turning things around so we get what we need can be as simple as being thankful for the knowledge that we are not quite where we thought we would be.

This knowledge enables us to focus on what we need to do to get back on track or look at where we actually are. Sometimes turning things around includes seeing what is actually there or happening.

Be grateful for where you are now. Look at the reality of the situation. Are you actually in a better place? Do you have supportive people around you? Do you need to take a step back and look at how you can benefit from where you are right now?

Do you need to take stock and make a change? Are you worse off or just frustrated?

Have you communicated what you need to those who can help you get there?

No matter what the answer is, be grateful for being able to be more specific and see where you want to be and what you want to get out of the situation, and see yourself in that situation.

This takes practice but the more you do it the closer you get to what you want and need being given to you.

This does work. I have a job where I help people. I worked out a way to help more people but regardless of my efforts I never quite got to experience that in the industry I worked in.

I did everything right. I put the work in. I spoke to people. I did study. I wrote proposals and training sessions. I helped a few more people but nowhere near as many as I had wanted to help and then I had an epiphany.

I began to be grateful for my current job and the people I was helping already and I began to look at new ways of helping more people. Millions of people and I remembered that I had done that already without realising it. I had written radio scripts which had been presented to millions of people and my work had been used in two different parts of the world. This set me on the path to writing this book.

My dream job is to encourage, enrich, and empower people and out of my frustration in one industry I have managed to turn things around and reach people through another medium altogether so I have turned around something that is important to me, something I needed to do, because I stopped and looked at what I needed, why it wasn't happening and was grateful for the knowledge that gave me. Remember what I said in the previous chapter. Never give up.

Owning your things

Often when we are growing up, in the workplace, in a relationship or are a parent we are told to take ownership, be responsible, and do something about it.

Yet in workplaces this is very hard to do in actuality. In some areas it is easy if you make a mistake I agree you need to own up and take responsibility but there are other areas where this is not at all easy to do and in fact openly discouraged.

You get an idea for something or to improve something. The company practice is to pass that idea on you are definitely encouraged to do that but what happens to your idea once it is passed on?

Owning your things is about retaining ownership or recognition of what is yours.

How often have you been in a staff meeting where you have heard a new proposal or way of doing things based on your idea? How often is that being used by your supervisor, your manager, and you are not mentioned at all? This is a common practice but one you can use to your advantage to retain your role in the actions of others.

If you give an idea to someone in good faith and it comes to pass under their name seize an opportunity to let the people above him or her to know where that idea came from. Do this casually for the greatest effect. Like I said opportunities arise it may go something like this "Bonnie can you catch up with David to go over the new system?" "Yes I can Bob I would like to see in more detail what he did my idea it came out of a conversation we had several weeks ago."

Alternatively with the advent of email you could send your ideas to someone and blind copy someone else, someone above the person you are giving the idea to. This ensures your name is linked with the idea and that if something happens to the person who is working on your idea other people know who to contact to keep working on or developing the idea. Your idea so they can come back to the source of the idea quickly.

I have learned over many years how to now minimise the risk of losing my ideas to promote other people in the workplace. It is theft pure and simple. Just because you can doesn't mean you should. If someone is trusting you in good faith you have absolutely no right to use their work for your gain without acknowledging their role in the process. If you are doing that now is a good time to reflect and stop it. If you have been used in this way, now is a good time to ensure you do not have your ideas owned by someone else again in the future.

Who had the idea? You did. It is your idea
own it and be proud of it. If it doesn't work
out that is fine you can own that to.

Helping others

I grew up in a small rural community on the
outskirts of a city which has since become a
part of another city.

I can still remember my mother baking for
those in need, or being a listening ear, or
getting in touch with people who could help if
she couldn't. Many people in the community
did that it was a way of life, but as the city
encroached and more and more people shifted
in the dynamic of our community also
changed. This happens it is normal. I can
remember when my dad had an accident at
work and was in hospital. A lady from the
church the next day to get mum to do
something for someone. My dad was
scheduled to have surgery that day, but mum
got a talking to about caring for others.

Out of the blue a lady turned up on the
doorstep to find mum quite upset and said
"Do not give that another thought I will let her
know and I will take care of it."

It was sometime later that mum found out her
visitor had phoned the woman concerned and
told her that it my mum and our family who

needed support that day, so she would do the task instead.

It transpired that this lady had thought that because mum was a capable person she could just carry on.

I am bringing this story to you because we are all guilty in some way for this thinking. We in the west live in a much more material world now than then and I often hear people say "Of course they'll be all right they had too much anyway." or "This will bring them down a peg or two." Let's look at these words what is missing? Compassion. What is present? Envy, jealousy, judgement and a lack of care.

Then there are the capable people who put others first and find themselves in a bind like we did. Something unexpected occurs and the expectation is you just role with it while you are still addressing the needs of others.

What is occurring here is an unrealistic expectation of you and you do not have to wear it at all.

When my husband was very ill we had well intentioned people giving us unhelpful advice.

"Maybe if you were just willing to let him go back to work and take care of the children yourself you would realise you can do it."

"Perhaps if you got a part time job that would help?"

We had three mortgages and three children under five and we were still a family if only just at the time.

These well-meaning, well intentioned conversations can tip families over the edge and are not helpful in the least.

Whatever coping skills you do have can be very quickly undermined and temporarily lost in stressful situations.

If someone appears to have more than you, or seems more capable than you and you see them giving to or helping others and you know or hear that something has happened to them or their situation which is not, such as a death, an illness, a redundancy, do for them as they have done for others and speak up for them if negative comments are made. One of things I have learned in my life is at times everyone needs the help, comfort and compassion of others at some time in their life.

Chapter 8. Material things

What do we need? Water. Food. Shelter. Clothing. Love.

What do we want? Well the list is endless and when we get something we want we either want more of it, we want the next model up, we want the next new thing and when we get these things on top of our needs we can begin to want and want and want.

Marketers love this and they help us pine and pander for more.

Am I saying we shouldn't have it? Of course not but if you can't have everything you want how do you feel?

Think about someone who seems to have everything they want, and gets everything they want. Are you envious?

We are competitive by nature and we want things that's the way of it. It is normal so don't beat yourself up.

Years ago we lived in a place where we were surrounded by affluent people. They had businesses, late model cars, their children were in private schools, who wore expensive clothes.

We on the other hand were getting by week by week and some weeks the milk was being watered down to make it last. Our income was meager but our bills were paid. There were no extras at all.

Then there was a financial collapse.

In December my mum sent us some money to get the children some Christmas presents. We went to a large store nearby to purchase the things on her list for our children.

We turned into an aisle and here was a woman I knew slumped over her trolley in tears. My husband walked on and I stopped to see if there was anything I could do for her.

"Tell me how to buy presents for the kids when there is no credit limit left to use."

I said, "How much cash do you have on you?"

"About fifty dollars." was the reply.

I suggested the clearance section of the store.

"That's where poor people go." she said "What if someone sees me."

"Then they will want to see what's there as well. I can tell you I get great bargains from there. Some of the stuff was just on these shelves a day or two ago. Who's going to know?"

Something else I've learned is that things are not always what they seem. Yes people may have more things than you, but that doesn't always mean they are better off than you.

Forceful personalities

I have covered this loosely in other parts of the book but what occurred to me yesterday as I was witnessing first hand this phenomena in action was this. If you have someone saying something that you do not agree with and they get louder and louder to make their point trying to shout out the opposition sit quietly, take deep breaths and when they stop to catch their breath state your case with conviction.

To state your case with conviction do not make the mistake of shouting louder than the person who has just finished.

You could start by saying "Yes I can see where …. Is coming from, however I believe or my experience would tell me that…."

Your tone should be one of conviction and your volume should be moderate.

Remember just because someone is loud it doesn't always mean they are right.

Just because someone keeps repeating loudly what they think doesn't always mean that what they are saying is going to be beneficial to others.

People can also be forceful by their presence. Some people can walk in the room and command attention and all those around them seem to get sucked up to the point they become invisible.

Quite often people with forceful personalities also have a forceful presence. I have often found myself intimidated by these people and at times embarrassed by their behavior. Feelings of wanting to become a ten cent piece and roll down a very large crack somewhere very quickly spring to mind. To be anywhere but here is another thought I have had. Physically removing myself from the situation is a strategy I have employed in the past but no more.

What we all need to realize is that we are as important, as unique, and deserve to be as valued as everyone else.

Quiet or shy people who get on with their business and do a fantastic job are often overlooked simply because they are drowned out.

I have been in this situation and it is not nice. I felt frustrated, all my hard work, my good ideas, hijacked then spoken of as if they belonged to someone else and the more I tried to be heard the louder the other person became to the point that diversionary tactics were added to the mix.

Diversionary tactics are when someone creates a situation or puts about misinformation to undermine you so they look better.

Be alert and be aware of what is happening around you.

Why is this person always having to get their own way?

Years ago I worked with someone who was just like this even when they weren't sure if what they were putting forward was right or not.

One day in the staff lunch room she sat next to me and began talking about how no one would sit with her or talk to her as I munched away. In the course of the one sided conversation she brought up how disappointed she was that people never took her on and proceeded to tell me how weak they were. The fact that I was one of those people didn't seem to matter at that particular moment. I finished eating and asked her "Why do you have to be heard all the time?"

"Because at home no one ever listens no matter how loud I get but here when I'm loud people just do what I want."

I remember thinking how sad for her that to be heard regardless of what she was saying she had to be loud at work. The point here is that being loud at home didn't work for her but as time passed I could see why she was one of six and her five brothers were much louder.

Sometimes there is a good reason why people are behaving a certain way. It doesn't mean they are right, but it also doesn't mean we should dismiss them as trouble.

In the end we helped each other and we sat and talked often.

Being thankful

How often are you thankful? I have always been thankful for things I have received but more recently I have learned to be thankful for everything. Even in the bad stuff there can be good. Not immediately perhaps but looking back over your life objectively you can always find something positive in everything situation if you are honest with yourself.

Take the previous chapter. I was the mouse in the room until something that was not good happened which affected me in a negative way and I reacted. Now the reaction wasn't good on the day and the anger and resentment at the time wasn't okay either but looking back that event was the catalyst for me getting help to become more assertive without that event I would still be a mouse. There will be people reading this who know me and may well think that I would make a better mouse, but then I wouldn't know those people now if I was still the mouse because I lacked confidence, didn't how to speak to people, didn't feel worthy of being in the same room with people and now? Let's just say if I am in the room I am participating well.

The journey I have to say did not happen in five minutes and there were days where I regressed but that is part of the process and now I am able to help lots of people speak up and be heard. Speaking up and being heard for the sake of clarity is not the same as acting out.

Supporting people

There are times when people we know or care about need our support. At these times it is important to be mindful that support does not mean overwhelming the person with help or advice.

I remember going to a woman who had lost her husband. I didn't know her that well. I knew her but at the time we weren't friends as such. I sat beside her for three hours until her family who lived a distance away arrived.

I sat and she talked and cried, then talked and sobbed and I just sat, said nothing and made the odd cup of tea. I felt absolutely useless to be honest.

About a month later after everyone had left and this woman was on her own she phoned me and invited me around for coffee.

I accepted her invitation and when I arrived at her house she gave me a big hug.

"Thank you so much for coming. I just had to thank you. You were such a help that night."

"There's no need. You would do the same for someone in that position."

"No I wouldn't but I will now."

I must have looked confused because she went on to say "I have sat with people over the years and told them what they should do and what they need to have ready for the family coming, and who to ring and I now realize how totally inappropriate that is. You were great and so patient. I need to learn patience." she said.

I was gob smacked literally. I learned something that day something I will never forget. Silence can be a great refuge at times for people. They can slip in and out of it on their own terms.

In my literacy work I find I often have to encourage people to speak and to listen. Many of my clients have learned to mouth off and tune out.

Isolating yourself from communicating with people is not the same as using silence effectively.

Chapter 9. Things are not always what they seem

I watched a public speaker one day giving a presentation and saw how he used silence to great effect. It gave the audience time to process what he was saying, it gave him time to relax between parts of his presentation. Throughout his presentation he looked relaxed, he looked open to his audience, as if he could be sitting talking about this stuff over a cup of coffee with you individually. He moved around the stage but not quickly, he used hand gestures, he laughed off some minor errors and you could see him as a real person. Was his presentation professional? Absolutely. Was it slick? Yes. Was he selling something? Yes.

I was in awe of this person if only I could do that I thought sitting there. While we were packing up I spoke to him and told him how much I enjoyed his presentation.

"You don't think the silences were too long do you? I have a problem with silence it makes me uncomfortable."

'But you use it so well." I said.

"Well I had to because I was saying so much so fast no one knew what I was talking about. I get that sick feeling you know when I'm up there that's why I use the gestures they seem to help.

I remember thinking on the drive home that there is hope for me yet and that one day I too could address an audience well, even with the sick thing happening in the pit of my stomach.

This person had to get support to be able to present well.

Supporting people is something we should all do as a matter of course. If someone needs help offer it. If they ask for it give it to them, if you can't find someone who can and will.

Supporting people is a very rewarding thing to do. Many people just need affirmation that what they are doing is good that can be the best support you can give anyone and we don't do it enough.

Life isn't a television reality show. Life is the real deal there is no rewind, no editing, and no fast forward.

If you need support ask for it. If you see someone may need support offer it to them. If you are not sure whether or not to broach the subject with them directly do something that supports them in a practical way. It could be dropping off a meal. Phoning them to have a chat. Helping them with something they are struggling with or giving them a helpful suggestion.

We live in a world where people have learned to make it look right. My world is the world of making it as right as possible for someone, because that in the long term benefits them.

Looking right. Doing right by someone. Yes there is a difference.

Life stories

I was interviewing a client recently a man in his early forties. He was quite anxious. We went through my questionnaire and he was extremely honest with his answers. At the conclusion of the questionnaire which he wanted to "get over and done with no good at questionnaires" I asked him if he would like a cup of coffee? "No thanks I just want to get my life story out of the way." By this time he was visibly shaking.

"Do you think it would help you to tell me your life story?" I asked him.

"I've been waiting all this time for you to bring it up." He said looking quite annoyed with me.

"Does telling your life story help you to move on?"

"Of course not but people like you seem to want to know it. You will have other forms to fill in won't you?"

"No I have what I need for now. Your assessment confirms you need some help with your reading. Your numeracy is fine. Writing will need some work and the questionnaire tells me how I can work with you to begin with anyway so as far as I'm concerned we are all done. Now would you like a coffee or are you a tea man?"

In my experience we all have a life story. We must have. We have all lived a life and sometimes that life has been full of challenges, tragedies, great joy, a whole gamut of things good and not so good.

This client had been in trouble with the law, had been in foster homes, had held many jobs, had been moved around a lot in his youth, had reading and writing problems and other issues but on day one all I needed to ascertain was how I could best help him with his reading and writing.

Over several months his life story came out and we dealt with that in a safe and positive way.

If your life story keeps coming up at the start of something ask yourself this "Is the retelling of the story helping me to move on?"

This particular client on our first full session did not have to revisit his life story once and we were able to start with what he knew already and move forward.

If you read a book about a person's life story like a biography or autobiography you are reading not just the life story but seeing a person who has come to terms with their life story on their own terms. They are happy to share it at that point and depending on the nature of the story to help others.

Being dismissed

Now I am not talking about being dismissed from service, or school. I am talking about being dismissed by those we care about.

You ring your aunt and she is busy and she says "I will call you later in the week." You are waiting all week and you don't hear from her.

You have friends you keep in touch with. You phone them but they never phone you. That is a form of being dismissed.

If you are asking yourself why do I bother? You need to ask yourself. Why do I phone them?

Dreams

Don't forget to believe in your dreams. Many people say "I'll believe it when I see it." I can tell you right now that is not my philosophy. I am the "believe until I see it" kind of a person and since I have changed my philosophy I can tell you hand on heart I have seen my dreams become real on a very regular basis.

My relationships have improved with people. My money is going further. I am receiving what I have dreamed of. I truly believe now that my dreams are real and the more I believe the more my dreams become real. I cannot emphasize how important dreams are in our life. Dreams determine our future. Dreams like love are tangible. We don't see them but they are there just the same and just as important. I see myself walking my property daily looking lovingly at my gardens, fruit trees, vegetable patch, grass and flowers, my tree lined driveway a welcome sight whenever I come home. I see myself waving to my husband as he tills the soil and prunes away. I see myself writing with a vista of colour and wonder at eye level wherever I am in my house or on my decking. I see myself welcoming my children, grandchildren, family and friends to our property. Having them to stay. Hosting barbeques and dinners. I see this so clearly. I see myself driving up the tree lined driveway and pulling into the garage. I see myself helping the grandchildren out of my new vehicle. I hear laughter and see smiling faces as if it happened yesterday, and yet I currently do not own this property, and I live 1500 kilometers away from my family. Why do I believe in this dream so much? Because it is what I want to have and I will have it.

How do I know? Well a little while ago the exact property I see in my dreams came onto the market in the exact location I need to be so it is only the means that now has to arrive and it will arrive. A skeptic would ask "so what then when that sells?" And my answer would be this "the right property at the right time is being prepared until then this is the right property for now and I love it as mine now."

Never give up on your dreams they are as big a part of you as your eyes, your ears, your thoughts, your plans, your achievements, they are you and you are them. Believe in them and they will be your reality.

Velocity

I was listening to the radio as I slept in this morning and a question was asked about the difference between speed and velocity.

Apart from the fact that I got the right answer which is in itself amazing as physics is not really a specialty of mine, the more pertinent thing is that I got to think more about velocity through the day.

Velocity is where something travels in a direction. We will briefly look at a bullet. A bullet is propelled into the air and travels at speed, but it really is travelling at a rate of velocity because the gun was aimed in a direction and the bullet propelled from the chamber and is therefore travelling in that direction.

For me the interesting thing this has highlighted for me is simply, when we get up are we accelerating through our day aimlessly or approaching our day with some direction.

Am I moving with speed or velocity? I have to say that on some days I have found it difficult to move, but as my recuperation has continued I do find that I am moving with more direction than just moving aimlessly about.

So overall in this context I would describe myself as someone who moves with velocity. The benefit of moving this way is you reach your goal because you know what and where it is and where you need to be to get it.

How are you moving?

Your past

Yes you are going along really well and then out of the blue something happens which reminds you of a time you thought you had dealt with, buried or shut away. All the old feelings come welling up, and you reaction to them shocks or surprises you.

The event is as if it had occurred to you just yesterday as if no time at all has passed.

What I have learned about life so far is this: bad things happen. Bad things happen less often than good things. Bad things affect us more than good things because they are bad and no one plans for bad things to happen in their life.

We plan for good things and the more we plan the more we look forward to them and the more we expect to enjoy them. Birthdays, engagements, weddings, anniversaries, births, graduations, farewell parties for colleagues leaving work or family members going overseas all good things. We look forward to these events and enjoy them. We talk to people we know. People we love are there. They are happy times. Great company, good conversation, fantastic food, nice drinks and we all have time set aside to attend so there is no rush.

Bad things on the other hand tend to happen to us. We don't consciously plan for them to happen. Once something bad has happened there is a process we work through to come to terms with has happened. This process can be short or long depending on what has happened and the person it has happened to.

Recently I was involved in a situation that had happened to someone. Several people were involved with the person affected and one of them said to me "I am sorry if I was a bit funny about that before. It has brought up something that happened years ago but it feels like it just happened yesterday."

When I was young around ten years old I had an accident and got hurt. My nana said to me

"One day you will remember this but there will
be no pain and you may be able to stop
someone else getting hurt because you
remember it."

When you are ten you don't understand that
but now I am older I do.

When something bad happens to you or to
someone close to you it is polarizing because it
is unexpected and usually involves pain of
some kind. Nothing gets your attention like
pain. Whether it is physical or emotional
makes no differences.

I have thought about this a lot and this is my
summary for when a memory resurfaces.

It is a fundamental truth that when the body
grows, growing pains are present, but once
you are fully grown, you get on and don't give
those pains much thought at all.

That is where your reality, and your capacity
to understand a situation for what it actually
is becomes beneficial to others. You
inherently know what is happening, you can
feel it, and you can offer practical help.

That is what you can do and that is all you
can do. If the person needing the help turns
away from it that is their choice, but they
could also choose to come back to you at a

later time for assistance.

For you:

If you have unresolved issues it is never too late to address them. Sometimes going through pain leads you to freedom.

"It is only when your past collides with your present that you know how far you have come."

Faith

What is faith? For me it is a belief in someone unseen as in God or in something as in a car engine that has stopped or refuses to start in some cases and you are sitting there and putting faith in the spark that will ignite and the engine going against all the odds to get you from A to B.

It's when you put your belief in someone even though you may not know them all that well or can see them physically.

Faith is a trust or belief when there is nothing to show or affirm that what you are trusting or believing in will a) come to fruition or b) is there in the first place in other words there is no evidence physical or otherwise that what you have faith in actually is there or exists and yet without it nothing happens. A conundrum by any standards. For me personally faith is what keeps me focused. Even when it never looks like something is going to happen or come to me I have unwavering absolute faith that I have it now, even if I have that faith for a longtime prior to receiving something, I always receive it or something better.

Our children have always thought I am a bit out to lunch on this but I have never doubted that what I know and believe is mine will be.

I know a lot of people who will state they are having or getting something and when it arrives they will pass a comment such as "I'm just lucky I guess."

Well I don't believe in luck as such. If you really want something and you receive it no matter how it comes to you or how it may look, luck probably has little or nothing to do with it.

It is your wanting it and expecting you will receive it that brings it to you by whatever means are available at the time.

Chapter 10. Love

Now let's have a look at love next because love can help you to gain what it is you want. Unlike faith love is tangible and you can see it.

Think of two people who are falling in love with each other. They spend lots of time together. They talk. They hug. They get to know one another. They fall in love with each other and when people are around them there are comments like, "Oh isn't it great they are so in love, or get a room."

Why? Because love is a tangible thing. You can see it or feel it.

Recently I asked a sixteen year old to do me a picture of a Kereru (New Zealand Wood Pidgeon). This young person didn't know what a Kereru was and had never drawn or painted a bird.

For three years I had waited for my request of a wood Pidgeon painting to be done. I never gave up and then on this particular day I was minding the students for tutors who were away and this young student from the art course asked me to look at a picture she was doing on a pad.

The use of colour was amazing and so I asked her to do my wood Pidgeon.

Was this luck?

I printed off photos of the bird and gave it to her and she sketched me a picture from the photo.

"Is this sort of what you want?"

"Absolutely." I replied.

So the background was painted but there was a problem. For some reason the paint on the canvas wasn't drying. The young artist came to me and asked "Do you think you could get me some pictures of New Zealand birds in flight?"

I was more than happy to oblige and did so. I printed off about eight pictures and there was one I really liked but I left it in the pile with the others.

The next day I had another visit "Would you mind if I did these birds instead of the one you gave me? I have painted another canvas a bigger one while I wait for the small one to dry."

I said simply "You are the artist it is over to you." The picture she chose was the one I liked two Wood Pidgeon's in flight during a mating ritual.

As the picture took shape the artist began to love the picture so much so that I had to state it was mine. She smiled "I really love it and I didn't even know I could do birds."

Then the small canvas was finished with the original bird and it was great as well.

How did all this happen?

Well I love Wood Pidgeon's. I saw one in a tree one day and they are truly magnificent, quite distinctive with their colours and they have quite a personality. From that moment I wanted a painting or picture of one to hang on my wall.

I had tried several times to have this happen but for whatever reason it looked as if I would never succeed. Notice how I have said that's how it looked. I saw my Wood Pidgeon's in my picture hanging on a wall in my house and when the right artist was available it all happened.

The great thing for me is that I got to see an artist fall in love with a piece of work they were creating. Everyone in the art room from the tutor to the other students saw it and it lifted the whole room.

That is love. Love is tangible. Love is powerful. Love can help move things to you.

How much love do have in your life? I fill myself up with love every day and everyday gets better. What happened with my picture is not luck. It is love.

What I have seen played out over and over again where love is concerned is this:

   "**Send love out first and good will follow.**"

I will give you a simple example of this happening.

Scenario One:

I received a phone call inviting us to our grandchild's birthday party. Now what grandparent wouldn't love to go? Of course we accepted and our grandson was very happy. Leading up to the party we were asked to take a few things along for the table.

We arrived early to help and we arrived with love. Our love went before us it had been active from the moment we had received the invitation. We walked up to the house and were met by our son who was happy to relieve us of the goodies we had bought as requested. He called and our grandson came next with lots of hugs and a huge smile, his brother and sister were lining up behind him and there were smiles and laughter all around.

We had a fantastic day.

Scenario Two:

I have been to gatherings where people have been invited to attend because it was the expected thing to do and those gatherings are often fraught with issues. People are late, food is not quite right, there are strained interludes, nothing is carefree and some people just want to get out of there.

I am sure some of you can relate to these two scenarios.

The difference is love. Give love freely. Be open to receiving love and remember.

   "**Send love out first and good will follow.**"

Heeding the call

Recently I was at a seminar about Education to Employment. This was run by a government agency for Providers of people in the Tertiary Education Sector. People who have left school but continue their education in a different setting.

We had three employers who gave of their time to help us understand what and employer needs to see on a CV from a person.

They talked about people needing to show they had stick ability, they could be part of a team and this became the mantra from them all the way through their presentation and the breakout discussion time. I was quite concerned about this because many of the people I work with and who come to me for assistance through no fault of their own do not have team experience. All the employers said they were not interested in seeing reading, writing or walking on a CV under hobbies they wanted things that could be conversation starters such as Hockey "How long have played Hockey? What do you like about Hockey?" Conversation starters something that would enable them to know a bit about the person.

I left that seminar feeling quite determined to do something about this and as I was gathering information about how I could help more young people be funded into team sports or situations I had an idea.

I decided to write to one of the employers who through my research about him I felt I could reason with. It took me a week to get up the courage to do this. I have included a part of the letter for you to read below.

I have done a bit of research about you. I have asked people about you as an Employer, sponsor, person in general, and I have to say I have had glowing reports about you, and the way you have risen through life to be where you are today. It is on this basis that I am appealing to you to use the subject of reading on CV's in a different way. To see that word the word reading, as a gateway to a conversation that will help you find out more about a person. You may just find that by saying "I see you have reading listed on your CV. Can you tell me why you like to read?"

Could open up a fantastic future for someone you may otherwise overlook.

I am going to share with you a true story to illustrate my point.

Recently I had a young man sent to me by probation who had a variable track record. This young man was never late to our appointments. He was always very thankful at the end of our time together and worked very hard. On our second session I asked him "How much do you read" he replied "I like to read but haven't read since I was pulled out of school when I was 13. It's 9 years ago now."

I asked him "What did you read back then?"

"I read adventure books. It was so great, when the bash was going down I could get my book from my school bag and lose myself in those adventures. You wouldn't have an adventure book would you?" he asked.

Fortunately I had some children's books on my shelf so I gave him one to take home and read.

It took this young man several attempts to finish the book and on our last session he said this.

"Thank you for giving me the gift of reading back, now even if I have no money I can go to

the library and get books and teach myself things."

This young man was looking me straight in the eye not at the floor. He seemed to have grown three inches. In that moment he had forgotten all about the headaches he had complained of for weeks from all the brain gym he was doing by reading.

This young man is now working and contributing to our community and reading everything he can get his hands on.

I have lots of experiences similar to this one that I could tell you about, but I have shared this with you in the hope that you reconsider your view on "reading" listed in a CV.

I went from being concerned for a group of people who are battling to get into employment to feeling empowered that if I could change just one employers view on one thing then the net would be cast wider and more people would have a more equal opportunity to get a job.

Has this worked? I honestly do not know at the time of writing this piece in this book but what has worked is I received an idea, I acted on it and only good will come of it.

How do I know this? Nothing changes if we sit back and do nothing. I have done something small as it may be in the wider scheme of life, but then life for some may be completely different because I did this small thing and if it is we can all celebrate the outcome because we are adding to the quality of lives for others and that is a great thing. Very empowering. We don't have to get the accolade to do good by or for someone else we just have to turn up and act. Fantastic. It gives me goose bumps as I write this and a very warm inner glow. That is why we are here. We are here to bring joy to others and in doing so are fulfilled ourselves to over flowing

Research

Given the times we are living in and the scarcity of work many people find themselves having to enter into new areas of work or new types of work altogether to be employed.

We have employers now who check face book to see what they can find out about a person and they are quite open about doing this. The Employer is researching you.

When you are applying for jobs you need to research as well. Research the company. What do they do? How big are they? How many people do they employ in your area? Do you know someone who is or has worked for the company? If you do talk to them, ask them about the company, find out as much as you can and include some of these basic facts in your cover letter.

When you are interviewed for a job make sure you can answer questions about the company This is important because it is showing initiative and a genuine interest in the company, it also gives you something to ask about at the end of the interview when they ask if you have any questions and nothing has come up during the interview. Ask them a direct question that you have wondered about when you did your research on them.

Research is everything in all situations I cannot stress this enough. Research gives you, a fallback position when things get a bit wobbly. You can save face if you have done your research yours and the other person's.

Chapter 11. Presentations

As I touched on earlier presentations can be a challenge for some people and let's face it today you are either watching them or giving them.

My "tech NO" label from many years back holds no bounds where Power Point presentations are concerned.

I have sat through those where people have read their presentation slides out diligently word for word, slide by slide, with graphs and tables that would have been interesting if only they had been large enough to be seen clearly, but alas the words before and after negated any benefit of this.

In fear and trepidation I found myself having to do and deliver a Power Point presentation. Lots of pictures on a theme were used and a few words. Lots of talking accompanied the presentation. My back up was large sheets of paper with the written information needed on them that I could pop up on a board if necessary. As with research I always have a back-up plan. No one gets to stop my message and I make my message as simple and to the point as possible.

Interactive Whiteboards, Power Points, Internet Clips are all great resources and readily at our disposal these days but useless if your message has not got through to your audience – absolutely useless.

Being prepared when you are giving information out

In everything stick to the basics and do them well. That is my motto. Communicate clearly. Sell or explain your topic. Get feedback on the way through. Stop and ask a question of your audience or ask for questions and don't be afraid to answer them honestly. If you don't know say so and get back to the person when you have found out and make sure you find out as you said you would.

I'd like to share a Math story with you.

When I was around 11 years old I was learning Math's and we were looking at Algebra. Our teacher got us to sit and listen to him reading out the Math's problem in our book then proceeded to tell us to answer the questions. No one moved. The silence was deafening. Not only was this Algebra it was a new topic for us. He looked around the room then asked if anyone had a question. I asked him "So what does the x stand for?"

He immediately directed me to the page and question number and read it all out again. I was none the wiser and Algebra is not a subject I do well or enjoy to this day. I felt humiliated beyond belief.

A couple of days later we were working away doing some writing and the teacher called out how do you spell Hindenburg?

If that teacher was before me today I would be very tempted to say go to the dictionary page 566 find the first three letters and around the 12th word down you may see Hindenburg"

How useful would that be?

Often people ask questions because they just do not connect with what is being said. What makes sense to one person doesn't always resonate the same sense to someone else.

What we hear often is not exactly what is said and for some people the words they read do not comprehend into anything that makes sense to them.

If you find yourself in a situation where you are asked to help someone please be patient. They may get it the first time. They may not get it until time 101. Never forget that you probably didn't get it the first time. Not many people do.

Being prepared for exchanging or receiving information

Always be prepared. This is the Girl Guides motto "Be Prepared" after all but what does being prepared mean.

When you are young it could mean doing your homework and putting it into your schoolbag straight away so that when you grab your bag in the morning your completed homework is where it should be with you at school.

Most people who are prepared manage to be prepared because they have a plan they stick to.

Being prepared and being organized are interchangeable and they are skills that are beneficial.

Being prepared can be as simple as having prior knowledge about something or having something with you that you are likely to need.

Documentation springs to mind.

I have a small notebook for my clients which they fill in with their full name, address, IRD number, phone number and other personal information so that if they have to fill in a form they can do so with confidence and a prompt if they are under pressure.

Being prepared can take a bit of time but save a lot of stress.

How prepared are you when you go to meetings? The doctor? Meet the teacher? Do you have questions written out to ask? Sometimes when we are expected to have the answers for someone else, we may find if we ask a question it can change the information exchanged significantly.

Take a few simple steps and get prepared. Several things will happen as a result. You will have more control over the situation you find yourself in. You will be more engaged. You will be more confident. You will be more relaxed. You will feel you are on firmer ground. You will get more from it.

"Be prepared and reap the rewards."

Validation

Paying yourself yes a strange concept I know in fact for years I have always paid the bank, the bills, the supermarket, in that order and many years ago the supermarket didn't fear too well at all.

Well I want to tell you about a book I've read that has changed the way I view, think and feel about money. This book is called "Born Rich" and it is written by Bob Proctor. It is free on the internet for you to download and read and it has changed my lens if you like on money. I now see money in a whole different way.

For the very first time this week I got my wages in and the split of money went like this pay us, pay bank, pay bills, pay supermarket.

I cannot tell you how liberating this has been. I am a creditor just like the bank, the supermarket and the power, phone, rates. I got paid just like them and I have put that money into a fund that will be there when I need it later. I do not touch this money it is mine to use later and it will sit and grow and I will pay into it every pay day. I am earning money off my money just like everyone else does and do you know what the best thing about this is.

"I feel valued because I got paid."

I can't explain how that has changed my day. For the first time I have got paid. This is not the same as receiving pay each week or receiving a benefit payment this is quite a different feeling. This brings about validation in what you are doing.

You don't have to give yourself lots to validate that you are on the payroll. Little often adds up.

It makes me think about the put yourself first debate that rages in many families and relationships which leads to the inevitable accusatory "You're being selfish" scenario.

Well this putting yourself first is a no brainer when you look at what you do for others. If you don't take care of you, how can you be of service to others? Serving others doesn't mean you do it at the expense of yourself. I have touched on this earlier in the book.

Look at all the very successful people in the world. What do they all have? What do they all have in common?

I'm not talking about millions of dollars or a high profile.

What is the first thing these people say when they are interviewed? "I have everything I ever dreamed or wanted and more".

They feel great because they have everything they ever wanted. They feel great and they go on to do great things for who? Others.

It doesn't take long to feel great about something. Praise gets you there quickly. If you have been praised for something you feel great. Why? Because you have been validated by someone for something you have done.

Imagine what great things you can do for others just by giving them praise. The cost to you is time. The benefit to them is incalculable. No money involved.

Moving yourself forward

You may think getting up each day and achieving your daily jobs or goals is not only moving yourself forward but some days a miracle. "I hear you."

At this very moment as I write this page I am moving myself forward.

Moving yourself forward is when you make the time to do something you want or need to do for yourself above and beyond or in addition to your daily routine.

Walking could be a way of moving yourself forward. Taking time out to read a book and learn about something new, or learn more about a topic you know already.

It could be going to night school or taking up a hobby.

Joining a group and meeting new people.

When you move yourself forward you need to put in place a plan so that the momentum isn't lost.

Get up an hour early. Turn the TV off earlier. Delegate a chore so you have time to do the activity you have decided on.

Involve other people by telling them what you are doing. You don't have to justify it just tell them you are doing it and follow through.

At work last week we had a discussion around an event that had taken place and there was some venting, brought on by frustration and all because a statement had been made, a group of people expected something to happen and guess what? There was no follow through.

I have to say we don't move very far very often we don't follow through. Let the detractors have their say. It doesn't matter. Say what you are doing then do it. Detractors can become supporters when they see you are doing not just talking.

Expect a great day and you will have one seven in a row makes a week. Don't forget to celebrate the good things as they happen no matter how small.

Wearing love

This is something I have just realized. Not because I am a slow learner or indeed because I am unaware.

Like many people I have been on auto pilot for many things I do. I get up in the morning and get ready for work. I decide what jewelry or accessory I will wear, put it or them on and leave for the day.

I am dressed and matched and ready to go.

Recently I was given a beautiful set of Jewelry by my husband.

This was completely unexpected and I was surprised and delighted. As a result I felt truly loved and this got me thinking.

I now change the way I look at jewelry and accessories that I wear. Even my clothing.

When I get up and get dressed I look at what I am going to put on and I only wear things that I love or that remind me of how much I'm loved.

I have a brooch our son bought me when he was twelve. Our son had gone off with a lady from church and worked with her for a day. She paid him $8.00 for his efforts.

On the way home they stopped at a craft shop to look for a birthday present. While there our son saw a butterfly brooch it was $8.00. He asked the lady in the shop if she could wrap it for him.

Now the lady from church pointed out to our son that the $8.00 would take all the money he had earned.

Our son said "Yes I know that but it is mother's day soon and I want to buy this for mum. Mum loves butterflies."

On hearing this the lady in the shop asked

"You would spend all your money on your

mum?"

"Yes."

"Well perhaps we could make it $4.00 then."
She said.

Every time I wear that brooch I feel loved. I
feel close to our son.

I have all sorts of treasures that I have been
given over the years. Treasures because they
are things given in love.

Treasures are great but I have decided my
treasures are no longer going to sit in a
drawer.

 I am going to let them see the light of day and
breathe life into my day reminding me of the
love that was present when they were
conceived, made or purchased, given and
gratefully received.

A treasure could be a bookmark made by a
son, daughter, a grandchild or friend and
given with love.

Whatever is given in love will keep on working
in your life as long as you remember the love
it came with.

I encourage you to see love and wear love
every day because love is always with you.

Chapter 12. Problems or opportunities. What's the difference?

I have been trying to find a good way of explaining this to people for a long time and I have muddled my way through the subject until this week.

This week I was in a workplace and spotted a computer desk which was the perfect height for a person to stand at and use a keypad and mouse.

I have been looking for the very thing for months and here it was in the kitchen of a workplace I was in. Do I ask about it or not?

Being courageous I asked the Manager when she came in what the story was with the computer desk.

"Well you see that's my problem. It was dropped off here and now I have to get rid of it."

"Really. Do you have anywhere for it to go?" I asked.

"No and that's the problem."

"What have I been teaching you about problems? They're not problems they're opportunities."

"Yes so you are saying this is an opportunity?"

"Yes because I am willing to take the computer desk off your hands. I will bring an electric drill on Friday and take it apart so I can put it into the car."

"Where's it going?"

"My place."

"We are going into town tomorrow with the Ute and I will drop it off. Problem solved."

"Opportunity created."

Just like that I had confirmation that when you look for an opportunity to meet a need you will have it arrive.

Years ago I would have put this down to being random but not anymore.

I needed a higher computer desk and have been actively looking for one without much success and now I have my higher computer desk without any fuss at all and delivered.

On the same day I experienced other great things happen.

I bought a side of lamb reduced by 30%

My husband won a competition.

Our son got a job offered to him.

My day was fantastic and all the things I received that day were beneficial, but they were also things I had been positive about and expecting a positive result for.

Be positive. Look for opportunities. Be open. Be persistent.

I am not physically in my dream home closer to my family yet, but I am expecting a positive outcome from a wonderful opportunity, and I will keep holding onto that thought until I am physically there.

What planet is this woman on you may ask? The planet that delivers and I am loving it.

Windows

Windows are useful they allow light and

information into our lives.

We can look out of a window to see what is going on and we can look into a window to see what is going on.

We can use the light from a window to our benefit by controlling how much of it we let in.

Curtains, shades, drapes, shutters all can be used to restrict the amount of light or information accessed through a window.

I was giving this some thought the other day when I was speaking with a group of young people. If they were windows the stories they were telling were quite opaque to what we had observed taking place.

How transparent are your actions?

How restrictive are you being with your life?

You see I have found that I too have suffered from the drape scenario, which became a curtain scenario and now I find myself in the full light because I have removed the restrictions that were closing me off.

Did I want to be closed off?

No and to be fair I never saw myself as closing me away. I saw me protecting myself with layers of coping strategies. These started with a curtain, then became a drape until not much light at all was getting through.

Now events in people's lives can trigger these defense mechanisms. I have had a few of those so I have responded as I knew how at the time.

What a joy it is to wake up in the morning now and look on my day through a clear window. No matter what the weather is doing I am surrounded and immersed in natural light and it is uplifting.

I carry this light with me all day and I find that wherever I go there is light as a result.

I no longer expect a bad day, or bad situation. I expect a good day before my feet hit the ground and I am thankful throughout the day for all the good I am seeing and experiencing around me through my window.

My window not someone else's window. That's the key. I control my own window and the view I enjoy from it.

I have found this transformational.

Am I being positive or negative?

Am I living in the present or the past?

Am I seeing what is there or what I think is

there?

Is my window clean?

All these things have a bearing on the quality
of what I see, what I feel, what I enjoy and
what I love each day.

There are days I have to get the cleaning cloth
out and wipe away all the redundant, no
longer required, comfortable thoughts and
feelings of the shaded days.

On these occasions I use a mirror. I stand in
front of the mirror and ask myself, where am I
now? What do I enjoy? Why am I here now? I
clean the window of the past by focusing on
what I want from the future and set about
changing my thoughts and feelings to get
there.

Did it happen straight away? No.

Did I get discouraged? At times.

Why did I continue? I continued because each
day I started to feel better. I started to search
for answers to help me feel and be even better,
and I continued on until I began receiving
what I wanted and had decided upon.

Of all the writing I have done over the years in
different situations I have never sat and
written a book like this before. I am writing

this book because I want the words I have to help people know they can be the best they can be. That is my job as a literacy specialist.

Do I help people read, write and spell? Yes

Do I help people use a computer with more confidence? Yes

Do I help people with their Numeracy? Yes.

Do I help people communicate better? Yes.

But that is not the point. The only thing that enables me to do all those things is by allowing the person I am working with to get to a place where they know they can.

It is easy to tell people YOU CAN.

There is a journey to that person saying and knowing I CAN.

I know this because I have been on that journey.

Telling someone you can is absolutely no help to that person if you don't show them how to do whatever the task is, and that is just the first step.

Step two is far more important. For step two to be effective you need to allow it to happen and not judge or ridicule the person.

What is Step Two? When the person fails at the task or falls over during the task. When all their fear and doubt rises up to the surface and erupts like a volcano and all the old pictures come flooding onto their mind. That is when you have to have a clean and open window. That is when you need to be transparent so they can see that you believe in them and they can do it.

So it may not happen the first time. So what? Just because it doesn't happen the first time doesn't mean it is not going to happen.

If Thomas Edison were alive today he would be saying each time it didn't work I could look at something else that might until it does. Thomas Edison gave us the light bulb and not on his first attempt.

Reading is like that. People assume it is easy to read so I should be able to do it.

Reading is a skill that is learned by everyone. It is not natural. We all have to learn the same way from ABC through to meaning.

People with Irlen Syndrome have a very big problem with reading because letters move on the page, but once they have glasses that correct this they have a desire to read like no others.

Their glasses are the clear windows that they have been managing without and their world becomes clear and enjoyable.

My window gets cleaned regularly and I am the better for it.

I hope you feel able to take a big step and look objectively at your window. If your window is murky I would encourage you to start cleaning right away. Doesn't matter whether you start in the middle, on the side, or in a corner, what matters is that you see you need to clean and make a start.

Your world view will never be the same again and neither will you.

You will see the real you. Get to know that person and allow the light to shine in.

Slip ups and disappointments

We've all been there me included and I have to say at this point that I am the best beater upper of myself and others.

At least I was. I have learned over the years that all that actually does is make you feel worse for longer and honestly who needs that?

There will be times you slip up. Just pick yourself up and determine to carry on as if the slip up never happened.

"Yeah right" as we say in New Zealand, or "like that's going to happen".

Let's have a brief look at what is going on here.

You have decided on a course of thinking or action. You start off with great determination and action. You go along perfectly well and then something happens. You revert to the behaviour you thought you had left behind.

"Really"?

Like anything we want to change we have an existing habit that we have been comfortable with for a long time just there in the recess of our mind, waiting, hoping that it is not forgotten or made redundant and with the right set of circumstances it can be re-employed and used all over again.

Sound familiar?

What follows a slip up? Disappointment.

Oh yes our justification for having slipped up arrives on cue with the disappointment kicking in and the guilt following shortly behind the spiral then complete.

For me accepting that on occasion a slip up

may happen has been the break through. When a slip up does happen I have a plan. I get back to what I was learning to do before I slipped up and carry on. I don't stop and think about the slip up as such. I acknowledge I have slipped up and I go to the next point and carry on not giving any further thought to the slip up. Why?

Well here's the thing. It doesn't matter what I do next the slip up has occurred. No matter what you think you might or can do you can never undo a slip up. It has happened.

How we deal with slip ups determines how powerful they are in the wider scheme of what we are trying to achieve.

Slip ups have the potential to completely derail your progress and your whole new course of thinking or action.

Likewise disappointment can attach to that slip up enabling it to become something more than a slip up, and guilt can cement it all into a problem.

Slip up + disappointment + guilt = PROBLEM

This is what we grapple with every day but the good news is this; we can start over at any point.

We can wait until tomorrow or we can acknowledge the slip up and resolve to start over right away.

Now this takes practice. It doesn't happen straight away in my experience.

The great news is that once you learn to acknowledge what has occurred and forgive yourself the starting over gets easier. Much easier and you find the slip ups lessen.

Slip up + forgiveness = Starting over (Solution)

You know if we spent just 1/3rd of the time forgiving ourselves for slip ups, we would save 2/3rds of our time by not dwelling on the disappointment and the guilt.

Slip ups can come in many forms but they can only stop you succeeding if you let them.

If they involve another person you must put things right with the other person as well as yourself, but so long as you keep putting into practice your new habit you will succeed.

Working things out

Since our car accident I have been reticent and not overly confident when I am at a Give Way intersection. I over compensate and probably drive all the people behind me nuts. This is an issue because at both ends of our road there are Give Way signs.

I recently stopped at my local Give Way sign and realized the new pedestrian barrier put across the main road was an excellent aid in my determining whether to wait or cross the road safely with traffic coming towards me from that side of the road. If the traffic is not at the pedestrian barrier I can drive across the road safely so long as there is no traffic coming the other way of course.

I can't tell you what a difference this has made to me (and my fellow travellers).

My confidence at the end of our road has improved exponentially and I am not exaggerating. Just knowing I have a strategy for that Give Way intersection means I am more relaxed when I approach it.

Now when we had our accident I wasn't driving, but the loss of control over what was happening has left its mark shall we say!

The Give Way intersection is a residual issue. I have overcome other limiting results and eliminated many other issues that were problematic in my life.

It is possible to be in a better place, or space.

It is possible to progress.

It is possible to laugh after sadness. Love after betrayal. Gain ground after disappointment. All these things are possible. What makes them happen though is you.

Look at the Give Way intersections in your life and ask yourself is there a marker where I can gauge is it safe to move forward.

Markers come in many forms. Body language is one. Feeling safe is another. Intuition. Never underestimate your intuition. Am I relaxed and at ease or am I on my guard? Do I have the right information? Am I doing things too quickly?

Look for markers in your life that you can use effectively to keep yourself safe, and move forward with confidence.

Chapter 13. Dangling carrots

This is something that happens on a regular basis from when we are young.

"If you wash the dishes for me tonight I will wash them for you on Friday night." This has been said by someone who wants their night off and is offering to do your night on Friday.

When Friday night comes around though that person is nowhere to be seen. Usually a brother or sister.

The next time a trade is offered by that person though you are more wary and likely to say no.

This is often our introduction to the "Carrot". The promise of something to happen.

155

If you do this ....

I think I have something else in the pipeline if you .....

Now for every one of these situations there is the person who is actively promising or inferring something good or of equal value is available.

The person who is selling you this needs to supply what they offer if they do they are not dangling carrots. They are being honest and honourable.

In a business sense Carrots are a good way of getting extra for no additional outlay but be aware of this if you genuinely don't have the position or the reward you are lying to people and sooner or later that brings your credibility into doubt.

"You should've known better."

"You should know by now, how many people have done the extra but only Dave moves up."

I say this to my clients: If it looks like a carrot it is one.

A carrot has two good uses it can be eaten or composted.

If you are offering carrots let people eat them

and enjoy their reward.

If you don't hand the carrot over it will wither
and die and fall to the ground as compost,
and that is where your credibility and integrity
is destined to join them.

If you are given carrots by someone else to
dangle and they don't deliver, all I will say to
that is make it a one time delivery, and send
the people involved back to the producer.

You see what we learn when we are little is
what we know when we are older. The
dangling carrot scenario is just this.

An opportunity realized and beneficial to both
parties OR people lying to get what they want
at the expense of another.

If you see the dangling carrot being used with
a negative impact on someone, or you see a
pattern of the dangling carrot being used in a
negative way speak up. By saying nothing
you are allowing the dishonesty to continue.

Likewise if someone comes to you and says
Jack has offered me this, and you know Jack
delivers on what he says, you need to
encourage the person to seize the opportunity
by affirming Jack as a person who delivers.

Carrots have their place, but I prefer them to

be in the garden or the kitchen.

Staying on track

To begin with and I am being honest, I have found this to feel like a fulltime job. I was checking myself and needless to say I became frustrated. Please don't put yourself through this.

Staying on track as I have discovered is as easy as being aware of what you are feeling.

If you say or do something and you feel not so good, bad, disappointed in yourself then that is the best Red Light you are ever going to see.

Think of a train running along the tracks. It picks up speed no problem, it heads in the right direction, it hits a tree that has not been seen in time to take preventative action, and it derails, big mess.

As simplistic as this may seem it is how we often live our lives.

Like I have said before in this book we are at times on auto pilot and if you think about an auto pilot it is programmed. An auto pilot does not see anything as such. It does not think as such. It stays on the course that has been set.

For us to stay on track we need to:

Be aware of the railroad we are on

Stay on the track

Keep our eyes and ears open

Look ahead

Watch for the signal lights

Follow the speed limit

Stay in touch with the people around us

How do you know you are staying on track?

You feel good about the decisions you make or
are involved in. You are not afraid to speak up
if something does not feel right. You feel good
or comfortable about what you are doing.
Who you are with. How you are going
generally. You are enjoying positive feelings
about things, positive outcomes, or progress
in areas of your life you have been working on
or thinking about. You feel happy. You are
relaxed. You no longer look for problems,
instead you are solution focused.

You know you are staying on track because
there are no negative feelings in your day or
your current situation.

Enjoy the feeling because the more you get to know this feeling the more quickly you can identify the things or behaviours which do not have you feeling so great and address them early.

The little voice that says "Do you really want to go there again?" Oh yes, we all have it and we ignore it at our peril.

The great thing about staying on track is that you come to realize you are the driver. That's right you and no one else.

If you find yourself doing things to please someone else, and you are not feeling happy about it, then you have not only left your own track, you have strayed into the unknown territory of someone else's, and drama will surely follow.

Read the signals. Apply the brakes. Get back onto your track and only deal with that.

As mercenary as this may seem it works.

You see the first person you need to take care of is you. The first person you need to love is you. Why? Simply in my experience because when you have you sorted and loved, you can love others and then there is a whole lot of enjoyment going around and it feels great.

Like everything new this may take practice but once you feel good and know you can daily it doesn't take long for this habit to kick in and real rewards are being felt.

Stay on track to your happiness. It is waiting for you to arrive.

Summary

I have named this book 'Airbags and Starting Over' and I hope you can see the relevance of the title.

Airbags deployed and shook me up, they saved my life, and as a result I have been starting over on a regular basis.

It has taken me three years to complete this book, and I am pleased to say the last few sections I have typed in. Something I was not able to do at the start of this book. I have had tremendous support from my husband in the writing of this book.

I have hopes and dreams still to be realized and I am quite certain that I will realise them.

Starting over gives us the time to focus on what we really want to achieve and therefore we have a much more targeted approach to reach our goals.

I have a plan for each goal I set and I work steadily towards meeting them.

I have enjoyed success in many areas across my life by doing this, and I encourage you to have a plan and stick to it if you don't already.

Nothing happens by chance.

Our accident happened because the driver of the other vehicle went through a Give Way without giving way. He drove straight through and ploughed into us.

Would I have written this book if that had not happened? No. I may have written something else but it wouldn't have been a book like this. I've been asked, why did the accident happen? Did the accident happen so I would write this book? No.

I don't know what the purpose of the accident happening was. Whether it was for our benefit or the other driver's benefit. I don't know if it happened so a lesson could be learned, and I don't waste my time thinking about these things.

What I know is we were in an accident and as a result of that accident I have re-evaluated my life. I have looked at where I have been

and where I am going.

I am no longer on auto pilot. I am moving forward with my life and enjoying it. It's a great journey so we may as well enjoy it.

I hope you can increase the enjoyment life has for you.

ABOUT THE AUTHOR

KAREN PIVOTT is the author of *AIRBAGS AND STARTING OVER and is a published radio scriptwriter with HCJB Beyond the Call with Ron Cline series 2001. Radio Southland 2004 and 2005.* Published play write "Gavin's 21st." 2000 Nelson fringe art festival and literacy specialist. Karen lives in Invercargill New Zealand with her husband. Karen loves educating and inspiring people to improve their lives and the lives of all the people they connect with.

www.ingramcontent.com/pod-product-compliance
Lightning Source LLC
Chambersburg PA
CBHW061722020426
42331CB00006B/1052